THE WORD IN AND OUT OF SEASON
Volume II

Homilies for the Sundays of Ordinary Time, Cycle B

by Richard Viladesau

Paulist Press
New York and Mahwah

also by Richard Viladesau
published by Paulist Press
ANSWERING FOR FAITH
THE REASON FOR OUR HOPE

Copyright © 1990
by Richard Viladesau

Library of Congress Cataloging-in-Publication Data

Viladesau, Richard.
    Homilies for the Sundays of ordinary time, cycle B / by Richard Viladesau.
        p.   cm.—(The Word in and out of season; v. 2)
    Includes bibliographical references.
    ISBN 0-8091-3158-7
    1. Catholic Church—Sermons.   2. Church year sermons.   3. Sermons, American.   4. Preaching.   5. Word of God (Theology)
I. Title.
II. Series: Viladesau, Richard. Word in and out of season; v. 2.
BX1756.V63W67 vol. 2
252'.6 s—dc20
[252'.6]   90-6770
                                                                 CIP

Published by Paulist Press
997 Macarthur Boulevard
Mahwah, New Jersey 07430

Printed and bound in the
United States of America

Table of Contents

This book is dedicated to the people of
Our Lady Star of the Sea Church,
Saltaire, New York
and
St. Brigid's Church,
Westbury, New York,
who inspired these homilies.

Introduction

"Preach the word, in season, out of season . . ."
(2 TIMOTHY 4:1)

"But as for sermons! They are bad, aren't they!"
(J.R.R. TOLKIEN IN A LETTER TO HIS
SON CHRISTOPHER, 24 APRIL 1944)

Most Christians will probably agree that Tolkien's exclamation remains as timely as when it was written. The fact that the father in England and the son in South Africa both had the same experience forty-five years ago that many in the church complain of today testifies to the fact that the problem of preaching is both long-standing and widespread.

Tolkien's letter continues:

The answer to the mystery is probably not simple; but part of it is that "rhetoric" (of which preaching is a department) is an art, which requires (a) some native talent and (b) learning and practice. The instrument used is very much more complex than a piano, yet most performers are in the position of a man who sits down to a piano and expects to move his audience without any knowledge of the notes at all. The art can be learned (granted some modicum of aptitude) and can then be effective, in a way, when wholly unconnected with sincerity, sanctity, etc. But preaching is complicated by the fact that we expect in it not only a performance, but truth and sincerity, and also at least no word, tone, or note that suggests the possession of vices (such as hypocrisy, vanity) or defects (such as folly, ignorance) in the preacher.

Good sermons require some art, some virtue, some knowledge. Real sermons require some special grace which

1

does not transcend art but arrives at it by instinct or "inspiration"; indeed the Holy Spirit seems sometimes to speak through a human mouth providing art, virtue and insight he does not himself possess: but the occasions are rare.[1]

There is no doubt, as Tolkien says, that preaching is an art (in the wide sense of the word), and one which in its practice touches upon the mystery of grace. It requires skill (or "art" in the narrower sense), insight, and virtue. But given the fact that grace presupposes nature and that arts can be learned, there is no reason why these requirements should be left either to the chance of native talent or to an unpredictable miracle of the Spirit. As the French preacher Olivier de La Brosse remarks, amateurism should not be regarded as a special privilege of the clergy; the art of preaching can and should be developed in its practitioners to a professional level.[2]

Theology and the Art of Preaching

In this development of the art of preaching, theology has a special role to play. On one level—that of content—the connection of theology with preaching is obvious. The concrete procedures of the two, however, would seem to be radically different. In particular, it would seem that the method of theology should have little in common with preaching. While theology has traditionally been thought of as a "science," preaching is clearly one of the pastoral "arts." Of course, if one defines "method" in a wide enough way—as for example in Lonergan's notion of "a normative pattern of recurrent and related operations yielding cumulative and progressive results"[3]—it is clear that the arts have their own methods, and are not merely the result of spontaneous creativity. But such methods are generally learned through example and practice, and their mastery has more to do with intuition and imitation than with the analytical and objectifying concerns of scientific methodology. It will be my suggestion, however, that the contemporary situation reveals a particular overlapping of theological and pastoral concerns, and that—the peculiar nature of every "art" notwithstanding—contemporary reflections on the method of theology are relevant to the development of a methodical approach to the art of preaching in the modern world. The homilies in this collection are the reflections of a theologian who, while primarily a teacher, has also been constantly involved in pastoral work, in particular the parish liturgy. It has been my experience that these two areas of the ministry of the word are intimately connected; that they are not merely complementary, but—in the pastoral conditions of much of contemporary American society—are intrinsically inseparable.

The Relevance of Theology

A significant part of the art of preaching, as of any art, is the mastery of technique. A major part of this concerns physical delivery: proper breathing and good projection, clear enunciation, pace, variation of pitch, etc. Beyond these are more properly "rhetorical" concerns like the effective use of pauses, periodic sentences, grammatical construction, modulation of voice, choice of language, and the various "styles" of speech. As anyone who has ever prepared a homily knows, however, the method of delivery is only the last part of the process of communication. As in any art, it is not technique but content which is the decisive factor; good communication is fruitless unless there is something significant to communicate.

As has already been noted, the content of Christian preaching will naturally have some connection with the systematic reflection on faith which is theology. Nevertheless, the degree of connection can vary widely, depending upon the context and purpose of the preaching. In some circumstances preaching is principally oriented to eliciting an emotional or ethical response: to comforting, encouraging, exhorting. In such cases, the preacher will draw primarily upon the poetry of religion. At other times, preaching more explicitly envisages teaching or instruction. Even here, however, different modes are possible, ranging from pure textual exegesis to the exposition of dogma. In the Sunday homily, which is our principal concern here, a certain variety and admixture of approaches is probably both inevitable and desirable.

At the same time, it must be acknowledged that preaching must take account of the difficulties inherent in presenting the Christian message in the contemporary context in which most American believers live. That context is marked by pluralism, secularity, and the absence of a Christian or religious context for daily existence. There seems therefore to be a particular need for a kind of preaching which might be called "foundational"—that is, preaching which speaks to the problem of faith's relevance (or lack thereof) to the contemporary situation. My suggestion is that foundational theology, which provides a methodical approach to exactly this problem, can provide the preacher with a systematic approach to addressing this need.

A seminary classmate of mine once preached a homily in which he began by speaking about the importance of the word of God in our lives. He had not spoken more than a few sentences when the sound of a radio became audible, apparently coming from immediately outside the windows. At first it was a minor distraction, but the volume gradually grew to a point where the speaker could no longer be heard. He stopped and stood in obviously perplexed silence as the harsh noise of rock music filled the chapel. After a few moments, the radio stopped, and the preacher made his point. It turned out that the whole incident had been prearranged to serve as a parable illustrating the situation that the church faces in general today: the word of God is drowned out by the noise of secular society.

The same point has been made on numerous occasions by the Nobel laureate author Alexander Solzhenitsyn.[4] Western society has the blessing of free speech. But freedom does not guarantee responsibility; freedom of speech applies to falsity as well as truth, hatred as well as love, shallowness as well as profundity. The result in practice is that every message of truth must compete with error, ignorance and shallowness in an uncontrolled intellectual "free market." In some ways, Solzhenitsyn says, this is a great deal more dangerous than the suppression of truth by totalitarian societies; for when truth is persecuted, it is all the more sought, and when spoken by courageous spirits it stands out all the more clearly against the background of official lies. But what can the speaker of truth do when the message is perfectly permitted, but is drowned in a sea of trivia?

In this context, the essential challenge to preaching is to find a point of contact for the Christian message in the lives and consciousness of its hearers. It can no longer be assumed that the message (whether biblical, dogmatic or ethical) immediately resonates either with contemporary people's experience or with an unquestioned acceptance of traditional doctrine; on the contrary, the preacher's exhortations will frequently be met with a (perhaps only half-conscious) suspicion of romanticism or mythology. As Karl Rahner has written,

> . . . until now preachers have usually taken it too much for granted that they are operating within the framework of the Church as something indisputable and self-evident, so that they need only set forth whatever the Church says. But nowadays, even in mystagogical preaching within the

bosom of the Church preachers are addressing people
whose relation to the teaching office and even to the faith-
consciousness of the Church as a whole is not as ingenuous
and naive as it used to be.[5]

In this sense the preacher today must proclaim the word,
as the author of 2 Timothy puts it, "out of season"—that is, in a
situation which is largely unprepared for and sometimes implicitly adverse to its reception. Preaching today and in our
society must be explicitly cognizant of the unbelief which is a
part of the context of each believer, so that "proclamation
'inside' should not differ now from proclamation 'to the outside' ";[6] that is, the preacher addressing a Christian congregation must assume that its members will share many of the same
unconscious dispositions, biases, and questions as the secular
non-believer of the same society.

In short, while there is a constant and shifting relationship
of preaching to theology in general, there is today a particular
need for contemporary preaching to integrate within itself the
theological specialty of "foundations": the attempt of faith to
"give answer" for itself (cf. 1 Pet 3:15) by an appeal to human
reason and experience; that is, to find in the human subject the
"connecting point" for faith. If this is so, then not only the
"content" but also the method of fundamental or foundational
theology will have a special relevance in the development of a
contemporary exercise of the art of preaching.

Method in Foundational Theology

Contemporary foundational theology explicitly aims at
making possible the communication of the truth of faith or
revelation to the concrete subjects of our society. To this end it
generally follows some form of what Paul Tillich called a
"method of correlation":[7] an attempt to find the correspon-
dence between the concrete human situation and the message

of Christianity. Human life is seen to imply ultimate questions whose answers are to be found in God's self-revelation. The "answers" given by God and preached by the church can only be meaningful insofar as they correspond to existential questions; hence a crucial aspect of the method of correlation is the analysis of the human situation out of which such questions arise. It must then be shown that the symbols used in Christian faith are the answers to these questions.[8]

A specific form of the analysis of the human situation in its dimension of ultimacy is the "transcendental method." Taking as its starting point the acting human subject, this method attempts to uncover the necessary "conditions of possibility" of our actual experience, in particular in every act of knowledge and love.

On a first level, transcendental method consists simply of the recurrent operations of the mind or spirit by which it functions on a human level. In this sense, as Bernard Lonergan points out, it is the "basic method" which underlies all methods whatsoever, and comprises the pattern of being sensitive, attending to data, inquiring, coming to insights, formulating them, weighing evidence, judging, evaluating, and making decisions. Its norms are not formulated rules, but the spontaneously operative "transcendental precepts": "Be attentive, Be intelligent, Be reasonable, Be responsible."[9]

On a second level, transcendental method means the explicit knowledge, objectification, and formulation of these norms. The procedures of knowing are applied to the process of knowing itself. In this sense, transcendental method is a philosophical pursuit which consists of heightening one's consciousness by objectifying it.[10] The results are the answers to the questions, "What am I doing when I am knowing? Why is doing that knowing? What do I know when I do it?"—or, cognitional theory, epistemology, and metaphysics.[11] In other words, transcendental method on this level unveils the basic condition of all human knowledge and responsible action by objectifying the permanent and invariant structures of the subject who does the knowing and acting.

The relevance of this method to theology now becomes apparent. It is "transcendental" not only in the scholastic sense of going beyond any particular ("categorical") field, but also in the Kantian sense of revealing the *a priori* conditions of possibility of our knowledge in general.[12] It therefore also provides an analysis of the anthropological conditions of possibility for revelation and faith: that is, the very structures of the act of knowing disclose the human subject as transcendent, or as "open" to an infinite horizon beyond the self. (Briefly, knowing is seen to consist in an affirmation of being; but the judgment of being depends upon an anticipation of Being-as-such [Lonergan's "notion" of being; Rahner's *Vorgriff* of being]; and the condition of the real intelligibility of every judgment of being is seen to be the co-affirmation of the existence of God as the absolute Act of Being or Intelligibility; a like structure can be seen in the act of valuing and choosing; hence every act of knowing or loving manifests and implicitly affirms a dynamism toward God.)

Critical to transcendental method is the performance of the subject. Because this method is essentially the thematic appropriation of one's consciousness, it necessarily depends upon one's having and adverting to the relevant conscious experiences. Only in the *act* of knowing or loving can its conditions of possibility be discerned. Hence the affirmations arrived at by transcendental method are in principle verifiable by each person through the examination of experience and its implications.

The turn to the subject as the starting point for basic method also implies the possibility of an "anthropological turn" for theology. Transcendental method shows that every statement discloses not only the object about which it is affirmed, but also the subject who makes the affirmation; that is, we can discern the conditions of possibility of reasonably and responsibly making such a statement, and the limitations of its validity. Applied to theology, this insight implies the possibility of an "anthropological reduction" of theological statements: that is, every affirmation about God can be restated in terms of its conditions of possibility in the human subject. This in turn implies that every theological statement should be capable of being articulated in terms not only of its "verifiability" but also of its existential meaning for human being.

Finally, transcendental method as I conceive it necessarily includes a dialectical moment.[13] This dialectic has two principal aspects: the contrasting of every theological affirmation with opposing positions, and the contrasting of both with the experience and performance of the subject in which it is grounded. Hence transcendental method is at the same time self-critical and intersubjective or dialogical.

It will be clear that this method offers a fruitful approach to "correlating" the affirmations of faith with the human subject as such, and hence is of great significance for "apologetic" or foundational theology. It is my suggestion that the concerns of this branch of theology ought also to be those of contemporary preaching; and I will further suggest that the theological method outlined here may be applicable—in an analogous way —to the art of homiletics, and that its characteristics correspond to the major goals of preaching.

The Goals of Preaching and Foundational Method

In his classic treatise on Christian rhetoric, *De Doctrina Christiana*, St. Augustine draws upon the tradition of Cicero and Aristotle to define the three essential goals of preaching: to teach, to please (or "charm"), and to persuade (or "touch") the listener (*De Doctrina Christiana*, IV, 17). For Bernard Lonergan, preaching consists in "leading another to share in one's cognitive, constitutive, effective meaning."[14] An examination of these three dimensions of meaning will show a close agreement with Augustine's three aims. Indeed, we may make a systematic and progressive correlation: a phenomenology of speech reveals that the sharing of these three aspects of meaning (in varying proportions) is intrinsic to all human discourse (this idea is explored in the homily for the 23rd Sunday of the Year); this communication becomes "rhetoric" when it is raised to the level of art; it is Christian preaching when that art is connected explicitly with the meanings and context which form the Christian community. It will also become apparent that Tolkien's three requirements of the preacher—insight, art, and virtue—are exactly the qualities which will permit the fulfillment of the three goals.

The Sharing of Cognitive Meaning: The Rhetorical Skill of Teaching: Insight

Human discourse normally involves the communication of information. When such information goes beyond the level of immediate sensible experience and involves understandings of the world, judgments, values, personal relations, it belongs to the sphere of cognitive meaning; and when the sharing of such cognitive meaning takes places as an art, one has the realization of the rhetorical goal of teaching or informing. In the Christian context, preaching involves primarily the cognitive meaning which is the "good news": the message of salvation centered in the remembrance of Jesus, and, secondarily, all the implications of that message for human life: that is, Christian theology. In this perspective it is obvious why insight is, as Tolkien points out, a necessary requirement of the preacher: insight into the message to be preached and into its implications; into the audience to receive the message; and into the preacher's own self in the light of the message; in short, theological insight.

The Sharing of Effective Meaning: The Rhetorical Skill of Persuading: Virtue

Human meaning is also "effective" or "efficient"; that is, it involves not only the passive knowing but also the active making of the world and of human life itself, in accord with our ideas and values, hopes and plans. To share one's effective meaning with others is to invite them to act in accord with one's insights and values—that is, rhetorically to "touch" their minds and hearts and persuade them to a certain course of behavior. In the case of Christian preaching, this means the calling of people to conversion and the life of self-giving charity in response to God's initiative of love. It is clear, then, why virtue is a requirement for the preacher. Persuasion is the effort to bring others to share the value of one's judgments and decisions, and hence is also an invitation to put faith in the speaker. But such an invitation can hardly be convincing or moving if one does not practice what one preaches; and, as the adage says, "actions speak louder than words" in conveying one's own conviction of the message.

The Sharing of Constitutive Meaning: The Rhetorical Skill of Pleasing: Art

Meaning is "constitutive" when human insights, judgments, values, in themselves create a new reality: that is, create the human world, the world constituted by meaning. Our interpretation of life shapes our conscious being and hence makes us what we are as human subjects. Our personal meanings make us individuals; our shared meanings make us communities. To share one's constitutive meaning, then, is to build community; for community is nothing other than the achievement of common meaning: common experiences, understandings, judgments, decisions, constitute families, nations, religions.[15]

If we understand Augustine's rhetorical aim of "pleasing" or "charming" the audience in its deepest sense, we will see that it has an intrinsic connection with sharing the constitutive dimension of meaning. Human dialogue in general aims at some kind of communion of life and sharing of the good. The attainment of that goal brings satisfaction to a basic human need and desire. Thus every communication in some way and to some degree affirms the other's being and contributes to the other's life. On its most profound level, then, the "pleasure" (or, perhaps better, "fulfillment") aimed at in rhetoric is not merely that provided by well-turned phrases and elegant discourse (to which the contemporary ear, at least, is in any case not very well attuned), but that of finding common meaning or communion of life. The hearer is "charmed" or engaged by a discourse which reveals meaningfulness and therefore beauty. In Christian preaching, the goal is the communication of the joy and peace that characterizes God's "kingdom." The sharing of constitutive meaning is necessarily a work of "art" (in the wider sense of creativity): not the creation of beautiful objects, but of ourselves and our communities. It should result in the joy of hope, the inner assurance of fulfillment of our total being. Art (in the narrower sense) is required of the preacher to bring forth that joy; the style of speaking (as well as the spirit of the speaker) must evoke and sacramentalize the beauty which it proclaims.

Insight, Virtue, and Art in Foundational Theology

The Christian dimensions of cognitive, effective, and constitutive meaning are clearly central to the concern of theology as a whole. The possibility of the sharing of these dimensions is of particular concern to the special field of "foundational" theology. While this theological specialty is not *per se* dedicated to the "rhetoric" of faith, given the situation of the contemporary world it is logical that the area of theology involved with believability should be especially relevant to the pastoral concern for communication of the message. That is, foundational theology is concerned with uncovering the "connecting point" of the message with its audience: the conditions in the hearer which make it possible for this message to instruct, persuade, and please.

By the same token, the attributes of the effective preacher —insight, virtue, and art—come to play a particularly important role in this branch of theology, especially in the exercise of the "transcendental method." As has been noted, this method consists in a heightening of the subject's own consciousness and an appropriation of its performance. While all theology should in theory involve personal engagement rather than mere concepts, this kind of method is more intrinsically personal in that it depends upon and formulates the theologian's actual *practice* of responsible faith: attaining insight, living the converted life, and constituting a symbolic community with others through shared Christian meanings.

The practitioner of transcendental method must advert to this practice and ask about its conditions of possibility. If Christian faith (or any particular part of the message) is the "answer," then what is the *question* in ourselves that it corresponds to? What is it in human experience—in *my* experience —which permits and calls for conversion and self-giving love as a responsible option? What makes the Christian message— whose central focus includes the cross—a source of joy and peace, a reason for hope, a revelation and fulfillment of our deepest desires? If the conditions of possibility of receiving a revelation from God do exist in us, then why is our performance so frequently at variance with its acceptance? What are the obstacles to conversion, and why do they exist? Such will be the kind of questions the transcendental theologian will ask in discerning the possibility of faith. It is my suggestion that the same questions could profitably be adopted by the preacher in discerning the relevance of the message to the contemporary congregation.

Transcendental Method and Homily Preparation

While it is beyond the scope of this introduction to give a detailed treatment of homiletics as such, it will perhaps not be amiss to offer some suggestions on how the project of transcendental theological method underlies the homilies contained in this book, and how it might figure in the concrete preparation for preaching in general.

If one begins with Tillich's idea of "correlation" of the Christian message with a human situation, the first step for the preacher will be to determine the content of the message to be communicated. In the case of the Sunday homily, this content is generally mediated by particular texts and by their liturgical context. This means that careful *exegesis* will ordinarily be a necessary factor in homily preparation. (There may be occasions, of course, when simple exegesis will suffice for preaching, but these will probably be exceptional. On the other hand, even when exegesis of the text will occupy a minimal place in the actual preaching, it remains the indispensable starting point for the preacher's preparation.)

The interpretation of the liturgical readings will have several dimensions. One must begin with an understanding of each text's words and the author's intent and context; but one must also go beyond these in one's understanding of the matter being treated in the text and of one's own context.[16] Furthermore, the liturgical texts are not read by themselves or in their original scriptural context, but in relation to other selected texts, with which they stand in greater or lesser thematic unity and (within that unity) in complementary or dialectical relation. This juxtaposition of texts—in the context of the eucharistic celebration—constitutes in effect a new "redaction" and brings to light further dimensions of meaning that go beyond those of the single passages. From this multiplicity of meanings the preacher must determine a theme, which may be based on one of the readings, on their conjunction, on their relation to the liturgical season, or on their relation to some extrinsic factor: current events, the particular congregation, etc.

The determination of a theme brings the preacher into the second major aspect of "correlation": the human situation to which the message is addressed. A second major step in preparation, then, will be *meditative prayer*. One must not merely read the texts intelligently in their context(s); it is crucial that one reads them "before God," and in the context of one's own life. Before preaching can become a genuine and personal encounter with the Christian community, it must first be the preacher's face-to-face encounter with God. The preacher must ask: What is the word of God being presented to *me?* One will find in prayer what Bultmann called the "existential imperative" of the message: the dimension of conversion or relation to God here and now that is implied by its acceptance. (This process may also imply the "demythologization" of certain texts: that is, getting beyond its objectification of the supernatural in finite terms to the transcendent meaning symbolized.)

From the act of encounter and conversion in prayer arises the theological moment of methodical *transcendental reflection*. Having discerned an existential meaning in the message, one may ask about its conditions of possibility. What is the "point of insertion" of this message in a human being? What horizon must be present in order to receive it? What does it say about the receiver? What is it in our common humanity which makes this message relevant for the author, for myself, for the church? On the other hand, one may inquire dialectically: What are the obstacles to receiving this message or fulfilling this imperative? What implicit presuppositions of my thought or behavior does it challenge? In asking about the conditions in the subject for receiving God's "word," one states its theological content in anthropological terms; one uncovers the "question" to which this word is the response. One arrives then at a statement of the message which is immediately relevant to our human being, which reveals our selfhood in its most profound dimension of possibility: its openness to God.

Finally, there is a need for *concretization*. One must find examples of the anthropological dimension which has been revealed in the life experiences shared by the congregation. Such examples may be positive or negative, showing the implicit presence of the transcendent horizon or its absence. It is here that imagination and "art" are crucial. One cannot normally take an audience through one's own lengthy process of reflection and prayer; one must find a dramatic instance which exemplifies the point in a way which captures the mind and draws its attention to the point; an instance in which the hearer's own experience of transcendence (or lack thereof) is evoked in a provocative way. Such examples may be stories from personal experience, or from literature or film, items in the news, occurences in local life. If they are artfully conceived, they will be more than a mere "hook" to draw the audience into the subject; they will be examples of the unnoticed presence of the transcendent dimension—at least as a question—in every aspect of human life. They should thus provide a basis for recognizing a point of insertion for the Christian message in the hearer's own experience.

In preaching itself, of course, the order of these four steps will usually be changed, and frequently reversed. One might generally start with a concrete example; then show how this experience implies a transcendental dimension in our humanity, a "question" about God and salvation; then relate this question to the existential "answer" embodied in God's word in the texts, leading the congregation to a disposition for prayer, reflection and action, first in the immediate context of the eucharist and second in their everyday lives.

It will be clear that these suggestions necessarily remain very schematic, and that they exemplify only *one* way in which the method of foundational theology might be applied to preaching. Moreover, this application does not represent a "new" approach to homiletics, but rather intends to make explicit what the good preacher actually does, usually in a more or less implicit and unreflective way. If my suggestion of an overlapping of contemporary theological and pastoral concerns is correct, however, such an explicitation may not be entirely without use for the development of a methodical approach to preaching, in which the insight, virtue and art of the preacher may more effectively be brought to bear on the meaning of the gospel in the goal of teaching, persuading, and edifying the Christian community.

Preaching in Ordinary Time

The homilies in the present volume of this collection are also "out of season" in a sense entirely removed from that intended by the author of 2 Timothy; that is, their setting is the Sundays of the year which do not fall within any of the great liturgical "seasons": the Sundays of "ordinary time" (sometimes called the season "of the year"). This means that there is no overarching thematic unity to draw together the individual Sundays, apart from what may be implicit in the sequence of particular readings. This provides a great deal of freedom to the preacher in the choice of topics—and also, perhaps, some perplexity. It also means that these Sundays are particularly well suited for the kind of "foundational" preaching which is envisaged above; for the absence of a special seasonal theme allows one to focus on the "ordinary" and everyday faith of the Christian and to ask about its presuppositions and its relation to concrete life.

On the other hand, the preacher is of course not left

entirely bereft of guidance in the selection of thematic material. Each Sunday's readings, especially the gospel passages, tend to underline a particular aspect of the message; and these are given a more general unity by the guiding concerns and special emphases of each evangelist. Hence each year of the liturgical cycle will to some degree suggest different directions in preaching and different examples and applications of the message.

The Readings: Cycle B

The readings for each Sunday of ordinary time, unlike those of the Advent, Lent, and Easter seasons, are neither selected on the basis of a continuing theme, nor arranged among themselves around a particular topic. Only at the beginning and end of the liturgical year is there a sort of thematic continuity, in that the gospel readings immediately following Epiphany treat of the initiation of Jesus' ministry, and those for the last Sundays of the year deal with eschatological themes and thus lead into the idea of "coming" which characterizes the following season of Advent.

There is, however, a partial harmonization of the readings among themselves in that the first readings, from the Old Testament, are chosen because of a relationship (indicated in the titles provided in the lectionary) to the gospel. Unfortunately, this relationship is sometimes rather tenuous, and must in any case usually focus on a single aspect of the gospel's message or context—not always the aspect which will be most prominent to the preacher. So, for example, on the tenth Sunday of the year the gospel passage portrays Jesus expelling demons, justifying his behavior with the parable of the strong man, condemning blasphemy against the Holy Spirit, and identifying his disciples as his mother and brothers in preference to his natural family. The first reading gives us the Genesis passage of God's condemnation of the serpent after the fall of Adam and Eve.

The obvious and intended connection is that both readings portray conflict with Satan: Jesus' exorcisms are seen as the fulfillment of the Genesis verse, "He will strike at your head, while you strike at his heel." Making the connection, however, means selecting only this aspect from a gospel passage which has multiple possibilities. Furthermore, it depends upon a use of a pre-modern typological exegesis of Genesis: for the serpent in the original context cannot be identified with Satan, and the identification of the "offspring" of the first parents with Jesus is only possible in the light of a "*sensus plenior*" which would need careful explanation. In short, attempting to connect these readings thematically—and with some responsibility to the meanings of the texts—might create more exegetical problems than could be dealt with in a homily of reasonable length; and it would leave untouched some of the more existentially relevant themes of the gospel. On this and many other occasions, therefore, the preacher may end up ignoring altogether the intended parallels between the first reading and gospel—thus leaving the first reading quite unanchored in the minds of the congregation. On other occasions, however, the first reading is a natural and happy complement to the gospel: for example, on the twentieth Sunday of the year the reading from Proverbs provides the text to which the gospel reading from John makes implicit reference. At other times, the Old Testament passage provides a contrast—either in content (for example, Jeremiah's excoriation of the evil shepherds of Israel and Judah vs. Jesus as the model shepherd [16th Sunday], or the Sabbath commandment vs. Jesus' freedom in regard to its observance [9th Sunday]), or in context (the legalism of Deuteronomy vs. a spirituality of interiority [22nd Sunday]).

The psalm generally expresses a sentiment which is thought to be an appropriate "response" to the first reading— or at least to some aspect of it. Here again, however, because of the very nature of the psalms, there is a limitation to the possibility of thematic complementarity. Frequently the sentiment expressed is fairly general in character, and is taken out of the original context. Nevertheless, the responsory verse may sometimes give a convenient and easily recalled statement of an attitude which the preacher wishes to evoke, and is all the more effective for having been recited by the congregation as its own prayer.

The themes of the second readings, on the other hand, generally are not intentionally related to either the Old Testament and gospel passages or to the progression of the year. We are given in the second readings a "semi-continuous" (i.e. in sequential order, but with large omissions) presentation of the non-gospel writings of the New Testament. In year B, the second to sixth Sundays are devoted to sections of 1 Corinthians (the remainder of the letter being divided up between cycles A and C); the seventh through fourteenth to 2 Corinthians; the fifteenth through twenty-first to Ephesians; the twenty-second through twenty-sixth to the letter of James; and the twenty-seventh through thirty-third to the letter to the Hebrews (which is continued in cycle C).

While there is, of course, nothing to prevent a preacher's taking the content of the second reading as the main theme, and on occasion it might be advisable for pastoral reasons to do so, it is probably more normal that preaching should be on the gospel. When this is the case (as in this collection), the integration of the second reading presents a problem. By rare coincidence, the passage may fit thematically with the other two so that its content can be integrated into preaching on the gospel without being forced. More frequently, the possible thematic connections are missed (so, for example, the celebrated passage from Ephesians on the mystery of marriage as a sign of Christ and the church occurs on the twenty-first Sunday, while the gospel on Jesus' teaching on marriage, with the Genesis passage on man and wife as one flesh, occurs on the twenty-seventh Sunday). Often, therefore, the apostolic letters cannot be explicitly related to the gospel theme; but, since they normally address concrete problems and life-situations of the early Christian communities, they may nevertheless provide exhortations of a moral nature which the preacher might simply advert to or use as applications of some aspect of the gospel message. In many instances, however, the demand for unity in the homily will preclude the use of the second reading at all.

In year B during ordinary time (from the third Sunday onward) the gospel passages constitute a semi-continuous reading of Mark, with the insertion of five passages from the sixth chapter of John (the "bread of life" discourse) in the middle (17th through 21st Sundays). A number of characteristics of Mark's gospel make it particularly well adapted to the kind of "foundational" preaching referred to above. The earliest and briefest of the gospels, Mark is less dominated than the other synoptics (and *a fortiori* less than John) by an overriding theological schema; much of the gospel consists of a succession of passages with little organic connection. The message is thus presented with a starkness and simplicity which challenge the contemporary believer.

The gospel of Mark emphasizes Jesus' function as an exorcist and miracle worker, carrying out the struggle against the powers of evil. This highlights the problem of evil itself, and the message of salvation as God's "response." While the church in our society is not in the persecuted position of Mark's community, the problem of evil in general certainly remains a crucial factor in religious life and thought, and provides a critical "point of connection" between the situation of the contemporary hearer and the gospel message.

Finally, it is well known that Mark's presentation of Jesus is dominated by the so-called "messianic secret": the fact that Jesus' messiahship is not recognized during his ministry, in part because of his own concealment of his true identity, and in part because of the obtuseness of the crowds and the disciples. Jesus' own preaching is presented by Mark as being "out of season" with regard to the expectations and mentality of his contemporaries. Whatever may be the historical accuracy of this idea, it can be taken as providing a parallel to our contemporary situation. It implicitly poses, in a graphic and concrete way, the "transcendental" question of the conditions of possibility for recognizing Jesus and coming to faith in him.

It is this question which underlies the homilies of the present collection. It is my hope that they will provide for the reader some insight and stimulation in his or her own encounter with the word.

NOTES

[1] Humphrey Carpenter, (ed.), *The Letters of J.R.R. Tolkien* (Boston: Houghton Mifflin Company, 1981), p. 75.

[2] Olivier de La Brosse, O.P., "La Prédication," in *Initiation à la pratique de la théologie, Tome V*, ed. by Bernard Lauret and François Refoulé (Paris: Les Editions du Cerf, 1983), p. 113.

[3] Bernard Lonergan, *Method in Theology* (New York: Herder and Herder, 1972), p. 4.

[4] See, for example, Alexander Solzhenitsyn, "A World Split Apart" Commencement address at Harvard University, June 8, 1978. Printed in *Vital Speeches* XLIV (September 1, 1978) pp. 678–684.

[5] Karl Rahner, "Observations on the Situation of Faith Today," in René Latourelle and Gerald O'Collins, eds., *Problems and Perspectives of Fundamental Theology* (New York: Paulist Press, 1982), p. 281.

[6] *Loc cit.*

[7] Paul Tillich, *Systematic Theology*, Vol. 1 (Chicago: University of Chicago Press, 1951), pp. 59–66. See also David Tracy, *Blessed Rage for Order* (New York: Seabury Press, 1975), pp. 79–80.

[8] Tillich, *op. cit.*, pp. 61–62; See also Richard Viladesau, *The Reason for Our Hope* (New York: Paulist Press, 1984), pp. 3–19.

[9] Lonergan, *op. cit.*, p. 20.

[10] *Ibid.*, p. 14.

[11] *Ibid.*, p. 25.

[12] Immanuel Kant, *Kritik der Reinen Vernunft* (Hamburg: Felix Meiner, 1956), p. 14.

[13] Richard Viladesau, *Answering for Faith* (New York: Paulist Press, 1987), p. 11.

[14] Lonergan, *op. cit.*, p. 362.

[15] Cf. Bernard Lonergan, "*Existenz* and *Aggiornamento*," in *Collection*, ed. F.E. Crowe, S.J. (New York: Herder and Herder, 1967), p. 245.

[16] Cf. Lonergan, *Method in Theology*, pp. 155–162.

First Sunday of the Year: The Baptism of the Lord

Is 41:1–4, 6, 7
Ps 29:1–2, 3–4, 8, 9–10
Acts 10:34–38
Mk 1:7–11

In recent years the world has heard much of the "theology of liberation;" one can hardly read a newspaper report about Latin America without finding some reference to this much discussed and controverted movement. We have heard of cautions from the Vatican and warnings from right-wing governments against its adherents, while among great numbers of workers and peasants it represents the true light of Christianity, and those who have died in pursuit of its ideals are venerated as saints and martyrs.

Whatever judgment one may make about the particulars of liberation theology or its practical strategies—a judgment which is made difficult by the complexity of the phenomenon —there is one thing which is not in doubt: the description of Jesus as "liberator" corresponds exactly to the thought of the New Testament, and is indeed central to the theme of today's liturgical celebration.

The feast of the baptism of Christ is originally a continuation of the commemoration of the epiphany: the manifestation or revelation of God's presence in Jesus. The baptism accounts are frequently read in precisely this sense: Jesus is proclaimed as Son by the voice of God and the symbolic presence of the Spirit. It is notable, however, that in Mark's gospel the revelation is *to Jesus*, not to the world; the voice from heaven is addressed only to him. (In Mark's gospel Jesus is not recognized as God's Son by others—even the disciples—until the cross.) For this evangelist the baptism is in effect the moment of Jesus' realization of his "vocation," and that vocation is phrased in terms reminiscent of the calling of God's "servant" described by the prophet Isaiah (first reading). (Note that the Greek word for "servant" used in this passage—*pais*—literally means "child," and can also mean "son.") Mark's baptismal scene therefore implicitly presents Jesus as the beloved son/servant of God, who is sent to liberate his people: "to open the eyes of the blind, to bring out prisoners from confinement, and from the dungeon those who live in darkness."

But exactly how is Christ supposed to be our liberator? Clearly, the doors of the world's prisons have not sprung open, either literally or metaphorically; and there is still blindness both of the eyes and of the heart. It is not sufficient, nor would it be true to the New Testament's meaning, to interpret Christ's liberating power in a purely "spiritual" sense—for example, freeing us from sin, but without changing the world (as though sin could somehow be separated from the conditions and structures in which it takes place). If Christ's liberating power is real, it must affect the actual world that we live in; it must change human lives. And in fact Jesus and his message of love *have* made a difference in the world, even though the transformation is incomplete and still underway. It is here that the theology of liberation has a valid insight: Christ's liberating power is not simply a fact that we confess, but is an imperative *for us* to become liberators, creating a world in which freedom and love are truly possible.

What does this mean to us? The task is clear enough with regard to peoples who are politically enslaved, or who are striving to shake off the bondage of economic and social and spiritual oppression. But what is *our* theology of liberation?

We must first recognize that we also are imprisoned, in

many subtle ways: in our limited and protected routines, in our insensitivity, our inability to love or be loved; in the walls of the defenses we erect, which become our prison walls.

The psychologist Ernest Becker has written in *The Denial of Death:*

> The child has built up strategies and techniques for keeping his self-esteem in the face of the terror of his situation. These techniques become an armor that hold the person prisoner. The very defenses that he needs in order to move about with self-confidence and self-esteem become his life-long trap. . . .
>
> How does one transcend himself; how does he open himself to new possibility? By realizing the truth of his situation, by dispelling the lie of his character, by breaking his spirit out of his conditioned prison. . . . In order to transcend himself he must break down that which he needs in order to live.

Because true liberation involves the breaking down of our defenses—including those that keep us safe from our neighbors' suffering—it is something that we cannot achieve simply by our own forces. It is only possible in its fullest sense when we can face death itself: both our literal demise, and the psychological death that comes with risking all, living in complete openness to others. The ability to do this is the liberation of Christ: the freedom to live openly, in love, because of the knowledge of the resurrection.

Second Sunday of the Year

1 Sam 3:3-10, 19
Ps 40:2, 4, 7-8, 8-9, 10
1 Cor 6:13-15, 17-20
Jn 1:35-42

"What are you looking for?"

These words are the first to be spoken by Jesus in the gospel of John, and they communicate an essential element in the understanding of the idea of vocation, the following of Christ, which forms the theme of today's readings.

As is common in John's gospel, Jesus' words have a significance beyond their immediate context, and are intended for us as well as for the disciples. What they imply is that in order to follow Jesus, one must already be seeking. We must not expect a call that comes out of the blue, miraculously and palpably, as in the story of the boy Samuel (first reading). The "call" comes, rather, through the recognition of the consequences of an inner drive, through seeking and then finding out.

This view of how a "calling" by God takes place—whether to a specific state of life, or to the knowledge of his "will" in our lives—has important implications. It means that we must not only have desire and good will, but also the courage to engage in the difficult and uncertain task of using our minds and discernment. A great man, trying to find what God would wish with regard to a vital decision, put it this way:

> . . . it is my earnest desire to know the will of Providence in
> this matter. And if I can learn what it is, I will do it. These
> are not, however, the days of miracles, and I suppose it will

be granted that I am not to expect a direct revelation. I must
study the plain physical facts of the case, ascertain what is
possible, and learn what appears to be wise and right. The
subject is difficult, and good men do not agree.

These words were written by Abraham Lincoln, one week
before his issuance of the Emancipation Proclamation freeing
the slaves. What is striking to the modern reader of them is the
author's uncertainty; it is remarkable to us that this move,
which in our understanding seems so obvious, was for Lincoln
a matter in which God's will was unclear, and in which his
action constituted for him a moral risk, a decision toward
which he had to struggle, without any supernatural revelation,
by using his mind and heart and courageously taking a stand.

Every form of God's revelation of himself to us, every
"call," demands a similar seeking and struggle on our part. The
disciples in today's gospel wish to pin Jesus down. They presume that following him is like going to any other rabbi, living
with him and becoming his disciple. Hence their question:
"Where do you live?" But there is no place where Jesus can
simply be found (the synoptics record the same insight in the
saying that "the Son of Man has nowhere to lay his head"); one
must "come and see," and "stay with" him (again, a major
theme of John's gospel that has symbolism which goes beyond
the immediate context of the incident).

Following Jesus means taking the risk of seeking, using
our minds and hearts, setting out on a journey without answers,
without a definite address to go to, but with the knowledge that
we are looking for something. It means then opening our minds
and hearts to the Lord whom we encounter in our search, to be
able to recognize that he is indeed what we sought. And
it means having the courage, once we experience that recognition, to "stay with" the Lord to learn what following
him means.

Third Sunday of the Year

Jon 3:1–5, 10
Ps 25:4–5, 6–7, 8–9
1 Cor 7:29–31
Mk 1:14–20

With this Sunday's liturgy we begin the reading of the gospel according to Mark. The majority of modern scholars consider this to be the oldest of the gospels, written between thirty to forty years after the death of Christ (A.D. 60–70) by a certain Mark, a disciple of St. Peter. It was apparently written in Italy, with the purpose of aiding in the mission to the Gentiles. Like all the gospels, it is based on the oral traditions of the early church, and not on the personal recollections of the author, who was not present at the events of Jesus' life. Its contents do not intend to provide a biography of Jesus, but a presentation of his message, illustrated by typical events.

Today's gospel passage affords us a good example of Mark's style. We are immediately presented with a summary of the essence of Jesus' preaching: the time of fulfillment has come, the kingdom of God is near; be converted and believe in the good news. The message is stated with urgency and in lapidary form; we are not given any concrete content, either moral or doctrinal, but simply the imperative to reform because of the nearness of God's appointed coming. The proper response to the message is illustrated in the next verses: one must follow Jesus, like the first disciples.

This action of leaving all things to come after the Lord is the core of the "conversion" Jesus calls for. But we are still not given any specific content to indicate what conversion or "following Jesus" means *for us*. Even when we have heard the "good news," and received the summons, it remains a task for us to find its concrete meaning in dialogue with God. We rightly pray, with the author of the psalm, "Teach me your ways, O Lord."

The center of being Christian, in fact, is not some particular content which can be isolated and defined once and for all; it is rather the spirit of "conversion" (the Greek word, *metanoia*, indicates a change of mind, a turning around). This is not an event or action that occurs once and then is accomplished (like "being saved" for some fundamentalists); it is a lifelong project.

It is true, of course, that we are already "converted" when we decide to follow Jesus, to make our own the commitment made for us at baptism. But that conversion is necessarily incomplete, by the simple fact that the whole of our life has not yet occurred: the future holds new events, new persons and circumstances which will expand and change the person I now am; and these happenings will not necessarily or automatically be in accord with my present or past conversion.

The person who experiences conversion or faith and wishes to "follow" Jesus is therefore faced with four possibilities with regard to the future. One can limit the future, determining in advance to experience only what is in accord with the present horizon of one's conversion, purposely shutting out anything that threatens it or goes beyond it. Or one can lead a dual life: holding on to one's conversion experience just as it is, and at the same time being open to new experiences which are not allowed to impinge upon it; thus one ends up living a divided life, in part converted, but leaving certain areas untouched by faith. Or one can accept new experiences and growth which go beyond one's original conversion, and increasingly find one's faith irrelevant to the person one is becoming, until finally one loses the practice, if not the faith itself. Or, finally, one can commit oneself to being constantly challenged to reconversion, attempting to bring new experiences into the field of faith by a critical use of one's mind. This possibility means the acceptance of conversion as a process, always needing to be activated and renewed.

It may well occur to some that what has been outlined here is a religion for the young. There comes a time in life when we do not want novelty and change, but stability; when among other things we simply do not feel we have the energy to keep turning our life around. And, in fact, Christianity is in a sense a religion of youth, at least spiritually and psychologically. (It is perhaps not irrelevant that its founder died before reaching middle age). The spirit of continued conversion is against an attitude of senility: the desire not to face anything new, not to be challenged, to have experienced everything already—in short, not to have a future, but only a past. In contrast, the "good news" of Christianity proposes to us an infinite "future"; it tells us that the greatest adventure is always yet to come; it makes us spiritually young.

This does not necessarily mean that the Christian's outward life must be in continual flux; but it means that the life of our spirit constantly needs examination, is capable of new growth in love—even new love and appreciation of the past, of memory, of our lifelong relationships, of our selfhood. The conversion to which we are all called is an invitation to make ourselves new in relation to God, who is always new, always beyond, and always calling us to himself.

Fourth Sunday of the Year

Dt 18:15–20
Ps 95:1–2, 6–7, 7–9
1 Cor 7:32–35
Mk 1:21–28

Catholics in recent years have been faced with a new phenomenon: public disagreement on church teaching and policy. For some years we have witnessed (and perhaps—if the pollsters are correct about the extent of the phenomenon—even participated in) dissent on the part of some lay people and theologians from teachings like those on birth control. More recently, however, we have seen in the media a rarer occurrence: public disputes among members of the hierarchy. The case of the schismatic Archbishop Lefebvre is an extreme instance; but we have also heard reports of American bishops outspokenly criticizing others over their opinions on how to deal with the AIDS crisis or even over the more basic matter of how policy on such matters should be arrived at.

All of this must raise in many people's minds the question of exactly what constitutes authoritative teaching in the church. The central point in today's gospel—reinforced by the reading from Deuteronomy—is that Jesus speaks with authority; and indeed we would expect, if God reveals himself in a definitive way, that this revelation will be authoritative: we should be able to look to it for guidance and truth. But there are several things that we should note about Mark's presentation of Jesus' authoritative teaching.

First of all, Mark does not tell us *what* Jesus teaches that sets him apart. Very little content of Jesus' teaching is given; it is rather the spirit in which he teaches that excites amazement. Secondly, Jesus teaches and acts—as we see in the exorcism Mark reports—like a prophet. In fact (as our first reading again underscores), he is presented as the "prophet like Moses" who was expected by many Jews to come in the final messianic times. The prophetic character of Jesus is significant, for it sets him apart from the priests, lawyers, and scribes who were the normal teachers in Israel. In short, he is not a member of the religious "establishment"; rather, he is inspired directly by God. And, like the prophets, he finds himself at odds with the official institutions.

Finally, Mark believes that Jesus' direct access to God is shared by Christians; this is the implication of life in the Spirit. It follows that one arrives at the norms of a Christian way of life by contact with the Spirit of Christ and by reflection. Note in this regard the contrast between the gospel and the second reading, from St. Paul: on the question of celibacy, Paul has strong opinions, but he does not try to enforce them or claim that they come directly from God; rather, he attempts to persuade his readers by giving reasons for his stance.

All of this is enlightening for our reflection on the question, "What is authority in the church, and where does it stem from?"

People expect the church—or, more precisely, its leaders —to have answers; but where do we expect them to get the answers, and who precisely gets them, and how does it come about? If we think seriously about these matters, it seems obvious that there are different answers, indicating both different levels and different kinds of authority in the church, which should not be confused with each other.

The eminent scripture scholar Fr. Raymond Brown tells the story of his speaking at a conference at the invitation of a bishop. Before the talk, the bishop lamented to Brown how poor his own scriptural training had been, and how he felt he knew virtually nothing on the subject. Yet when he introduced the speaker, he pointedly told the audience to remember that anything they might hear was only scholarly opinion, and that only bishops can rightly interpret the scriptures.

Are Catholics supposed to think, then, that there are some people in the church who obtain an expertise in scripture or in theology directly from above, by divine inspiration, and without having to study or engage in scholarship? If this were the case, why should anyone bother to do the hard work of studying, when a superior result could be obtained simply by episcopal ordination? And, if this were the case, how could the inspired authorities disagree with each other?

It is clear that this is not the nature of the church's claim to authoritative teaching; a distinction is necessary. One kind of authority is that of expertise. Theologians do not claim divine inspiration and do not argue on the basis of their status. They present reasons for their conclusions. This kind of authority, which argues and appeals to our intelligence, must necessarily be open to dialogue, advance, and change.

There is another kind of authority, however, which is concerned with overseeing, pastoral care, direction and leadership. It also must necessarily teach. But its bearers cannot claim expertise, unless they have gained it in the usual way; they must depend upon others—the theological tradition and present theology—for the theological or scriptural basis of their statements. It is this kind of authority which is exercised by the hierarchy.

This second form of authority does depend upon a charism or an inspiration. But it also must be open to dialogue. For, if we take seriously the gospel message, we must hold that the spirit of prophecy, the spirit of Christ, is in *all* his people, even if not all have the same function in the community.

The praying of the eucharist gives us an example of the two dimensions of authority in the church interacting. In preaching, the priest speaks to the congregation, on the basis (one hopes) of his knowledge and training. In the eucharistic prayer, however, he speaks *for* the congregation, as the one appointed to speak on behalf of the whole Spirit-filled people. We should be able to expect that the pastoral office of the church in general should reflect this structure of the church at prayer: our leaders are not above the church, but a specially functioning part of the whole to which we all belong.

Fifth Sunday of the Year

Jb 7:1–4, 6–7
Ps 147:1–2, 3–4, 5–6
1 Cor 9:16–19, 22–23
Mk 1:29–39

There is probably no one among us who has not at some time had the experience of being ill. It is clear, if we think about it, that sickness is not experienced simply as a physical condition. It is also a form of alienation; we have a sense of "wrongness" about our state of being. Human life only makes sense if we can live well and be happy; we have a deep-seated feeling that a state of misery or an embattled, threatened state of being is not only subjectively painful, but is objectively "wrong"; it ought not to be so.

Those who are seriously sick frequently turn to God—not simply in the hope of getting well, although this is certainly foremost in most people's minds, but also because sickness brings to our consciousness a perspective on the meaning of life itself. In sickness we experience life's fragility, its loneliness and lack of peace; and we recognize that these are aspects of the human condition in general, although they are frequently hidden and ignored when we are in a state of physical health and "normalcy."

The connection of sickness with our spiritual state gives healing a special significance; it becomes a sign of something greater. Jesus' healings in particular are presented as signs of God's kingdom: not merely acts of power for a particular individual, but indications of a transformation of the whole threatened and alienated human condition. The biblical understand-

37

ing of healings as the casting out of demons makes sense even to us on the level of image: sickness is experienced as an alien power, and getting well is like winning a battle over evil forces. The image is even more powerful when we think of healing not merely as a physical event, but as a sign of God's victory over evil in general.

The healings of Jesus, then, are not performed simply for their own sake, but as the physical manifestation of what Jesus preaches: the coming kingdom of God and the human response of conversion. Jesus' mission, as he says in today's gospel, is essentially to preach, not to be a healer; the cures he works are intended to show that the power we turn to in illness is in fact at work in the world, and is giving health not merely physically, but is healing life itself, giving it meaning and purpose.

Most of us have experienced healing on both of these levels. We know how wonderful it is when a demon is cast out—when health is restored by medicine, or when hope and meaning are restored by conversion and love. We see healing as sacred; we honor both medical and psychological doctors and healers of the soul. We consider the care of the sick to be honorable and admirable; we feel horror at those societies where the sick are neglected or even cast out.

But there is another dimension to sickness that we do not so easily attend to. There is sickness and alienation in society as well as in individuals. Whole groups of people are dis-related to the public body. One sad example is the increasing number of the jobless and homeless in so many of our cities: people caught in misfortune and then subjected to public hostility and to a social system which frequently intensifies their problems. The solution to such social sickness can only be societal; yet our society seems to be turning away from the task of healing. Many studies have documented the growing gap between the new affluence and the new poverty in our midst. But the fortunate seem not to want to be concerned. In the years since 1980, many social assistance programs have been radically reduced. Society seems embarrassed by those who remind us of the fragility of life and our embattled state.

On yet another level, there are the worldwide problems of poverty, hunger, underdevelopment, and the gap between rich and poor nations. Whole areas of the globe are languishing as though in disease.

Is there hope for healing? What is needed is a conversion of values on a large scale. Churches are among the most active in meeting the problems and in spreading concern; but clearly private charity cannot resolve such public and widespread ailments. Perhaps there is hope that the attitudes of Christians can help to change the mind and heart of our society as a whole, to make its priorities those symbolized by Jesus' healings.

When we are sick, we have a clear vision of what is important and what is superficial and trivial. Too frequently we lose that vision when we feel ourselves in health. Our task as Christians is to give others that vision by living it in our own lives.

Sixth Sunday of the Year

Lev 13:1–2, 44–46
Ps 32:1–2, 5, 11
1 Cor 10:31–11:1
Mk 1:40–45

E. M. Forster wrote: "Only connect. . . ." If only we could connect with each other, how different would our world be! Every so often I receive letters from classmates who are missionaries in remote and undeveloped parts of Latin America. They create for me a connection between abstract notions like deficit, trade balance, ecology, and the concrete realities of people in the third world who lead lives of suffering and pain because of our way of living in the prosperous part of this globe. Realities which are outside the limits of the considerations of daily concerns are suddenly connected with my life through people I know and care about.

Today's gospel also has to do with making connection with the disconnected. Leprosy was for the ancient Jews a symbol of "sin" in the sense of alienation: lepers constituted a sphere outside the community and outside the law; they were beyond the pale of humanity and of God's dealings. Leprosy was something people could not deal with (the rabbis held that curing leprosy was as difficult as raising the dead), and thus had to protect themselves from it. It was a supreme symbol of the dangerous.

Jesus' action in the gospel signifies that God's power reaches even into this situation: it saves what is beyond the law and human power; it enters into the most alienated and dangerous areas. Nothing is beyond the pale of God's love and power.

(The same symbol is repeated in the lives of the saints: think of St. Francis forcing himself to serve and to kiss the leper.)

The reading from St. Paul also has to do with making connections. He tells the Corinthians: "Whether you eat or drink, or whatever you do, do it to the glory of God . . ." The context is the question of pure and impure foods. Can Christians eat meat which has been slaughtered in the ritual of sacrifice to the pagan gods (as would be the case with much of the meat in the markets)? For the Jewish mentality, this was another area beyond the law and relation with God, a sphere of danger. Paul answers: there is no law about what you eat; but there are connections to be made. The Christian must connect with other people's consciences, even if he or she is quite at ease; we must act for God's "glory," which consists in mutual harmony and love. Nothing in itself is beyond the pale of God's glory—if only we connect.

God's reaching into the dangerous areas gives us courage to face them in ourselves: courage to face our insecurities, inadequacies, and fears; courage to face the horrid countenance of sin; even death. It also gives us an example: we must also connect with the "lepers" of the world—those who are outside the pale of our thought and concern, the disconnected.

It is important for us to recognize both aspects of the message: the comfort and the demand. Religion is meant to make connections (some even derive the word etymologically from the Latin word for "tying together"); yet we can sacralize, liturgicize, sanitize our religion, making salvation something clean and neat and comfortable, and never touching upon exactly those areas that need to be saved.

Today's gospel text contains a number of ambiguities. Many of the best Greek manuscripts tell us that Jesus "got angry" (*orgistheis*) with the leper rather than "had pity" (*splagchnistheis*); the Syriac text also has the former sense. Furthermore, the word which our version translates as "gave a stern warning" (*embrimesamenos*) is actually much stronger in Greek: it means to rebuke (the Syriac has a word meaning "to wound verbally, to terrify"). And where our translation says Jesus "sent him on his way," the Greek says *ekbalen auton:* "cast him out." All this leads us to suspect that behind our present text we can discern an earlier version, in which Jesus acts as an exorcist, addressing not the leper, but the leprosy: getting angry at, rebuking, casting out the force of evil personified as a demon.

This reading of the text gives us a rather different picture of Jesus: not an omnipotent figure, above the battle, condescending and feeling only pity—the sentiment of a superior being for an inferior; but rather involved in the battle, feeling angry passion against evil, feeling its threat; being connected. This image of Jesus, which comes forth in a number of passages, particularly in the synoptics, has frequently been obscured by the glorifications of piety. It is important, because it reminds us that Jesus is not merely a medium for the omnipotence of God to enter the world, condescending, and work for us, but that he is a human being, and the model of how we are to work for each other; he is connected with our lives and struggles.

The eucharist tells us each time we celebrate it that the life and death of a man who lived nearly two thousand years ago is really connected with ours, because Jesus made the ultimate connection—that of love—to the point of dying for it. Our faith in that connection is real, because God's love is real, and reaches everywhere; the condition is that we only connect.

Seventh Sunday of the Year

Is 43:18–19, 21–22, 24–25
Ps 41:2–3, 4–5, 13–14
2 Cor 1:18–22
Mk 2:1–12

"Which is easier, to say to the paralytic, 'Your sins are forgiven,' or to say, 'Stand up, pick up your mat, and walk again?'"

In the context of the story, Jesus' question seems to build upon a purposeful ambiguity, based on the contrast between appearance and reality. In appearance, if one claims that someone's sins are forgiven, there is no way of verifying or falsifying the statement, whereas a claim to heal can immediately be tested. Therefore it appears (to the scribes) that it is easier to *say,* "Your sins are forgiven." But in reality, it is the forgiveness of sins which is the much greater work, for as the scribes themselves think, no one can forgive sins but God alone. Therefore it seems to the skeptical scribes that Jesus is making an enormous, impossible claim—to declare the forgiveness of sins—but one which is easy for him to make, since there is no way to disprove it.

Jesus, however, cuts through their skepticism by offering a sign. He does what seems to be the harder thing: gives a visible, verifiable instance of his power. In fact, the healing of the paralytic is intended to be seen in faith as the extension into the physical world of the forgiveness and spiritual healing which Jesus had already proclaimed. Mark has already made it clear in the first chapter of his gospel (which we have heard in previous Sundays) that Jesus is God's messiah, the bringer of the kingdom; in his works, that kingdom already breaks forth into the world by the healing of ills and the expulsion of the powers of evil.

We, of course, have long since heard and believed in Jesus' message. How would *we* answer his question to the scribes in today's gospel story? Which is easier—physical healing, or the forgiveness of sins?

For some generations, the Christian message was presented with such emphasis on human sinfulness and the need for obedience to God's precepts that his love and forgiveness were nearly forgotten. God was seen as the just judge, before whom even the righteous will scarcely be secure on the day of judgment (as is explicitly stated in the text of the ancient funeral sequence, the *Dies Irae*). The forgiveness of sins was seen as something difficult, something to be attended to and worked at with at least as much diligence as one would attend to seeking a cure for physical illness.

In our day, we have lived through a happy renewal of the church, in which we have heard more clearly the positive side of the message of Jesus, the "good news" of God's all-embracing love and forgiveness.

But there is a danger if we think that the forgiveness of sins is simply something "easy"—if we presume that we are always forgiven automatically, or that forgiveness does not need to be attended to.

In today's gospel story, Mark makes it clear that Jesus' words of forgiveness and of healing are a response to *faith*. This is always the case with Jesus' works, whether spiritual or physical. There is a desire on the part of the recipient, a readiness to be healed and reconciled. (In this gospel passage, the faith explicitly referred to is that of the friends of the paralytic —a reminder of the communal dimension of faith). Without this receptivity, Jesus' action cannot take place (cf. Mk 6:5).

A danger of living in a permissive and self-indulgent society like our own is that we may unconsciously adopt some of its fundamental attitudes; we may become easy on ourselves, and neglect to take seriously the need of faith—which to be alive must be a vital and active relationship of love. We may too easily overlook our own failings, and presume God's forgiveness without the attitude on our part that makes it possible.

It is true, as we hear in the second reading, that God's word to us is not sometimes "yes" and sometimes "no"; God's love is constant, and so also is his desire to forgive and reconcile us to himself. But reconciliation demands a change on our part. Forgiveness, after all, does not simply mean amnesty; it is not simply a matter of declaring that we will not have to "pay" for our wrongdoing. Sin, in its essence, is something wrong *in us*, in our "heart," not merely in our behavior; and forgiveness necessarily means a change of heart. In short, the message of forgiveness is intimately tied to Jesus' central imperative: conversion. To be forgiven is to be converted by God's all-embracing love into one who loves like God.

Eighth Sunday of the Year

Hos 2:16, 17, 21–22
Ps 103:1–2, 3–4, 8, 10, 12–13
2 Cor 3:1–6
Mk 2:18–22

"For new wine, new wineskins!"

Every passage in the gospels can be read in at least three contexts:

(1) the context in Jesus' life: what actually took place, and what did it mean to Jesus and those around him?

(2) the context in the life of the early church (the oral tradition passing on the story) and of the evangelist: what did the event and/or saying mean to the community from which the evangelist received them? how did the evangelist reinterpret this understanding? why does he narrate the event, and what message is it intended to convey to the community he writes for?

(3) the context in *our* lives: what does this passage say to us—about faith, about our relation to God, about the meaning of life?

For today's gospel passage, the meaning in the first two contexts is fairly easy to find. It concerns the irreconcilability of the new with the old, symbolized by fermenting wine in dry skins or an unshrunken patch on an already shrunken garment. For Jesus, the new wine or new cloth is the kingdom of God, presented in his preaching; it cannot be accepted as long as one clings to the old way of life. It demands *total* reform; one can only accept Jesus on condition of complete conversion.

Mark, on the other hand, presents these sayings in the

context of the relationship of Christianity to Judaism. He places them after a discussion of fasting, a practice of the Jewish community. His message is that the new community cannot live by the old laws and practices: Judaism has been surpassed by a new community, the eschatological community, that of Christ.

But what can these sayings mean to *us?* How can the message of Jesus still be "new wine" after nearly two thousand years?

The message of Jesus has become part of the history of the world; it has not only given rise to institutional form in the church, but has profoundly affected the entire western worldview. It is difficult to think of these ideas as new. This is especially true for us who are lifelong Christians. Jesus' hearers were people who encountered him and his teaching for the first time; Mark's Christians were of the first or second generation, converts from a Jewish or pagan background; but most of us were brought up on Christianity. Its teachings are not news to us, but are what has shaped our lives from the beginning. The gospel seems to many in our situation more like old wine or an old garment than new.

To find a significance for us in Jesus' statement in this passage, we must look more closely at the meaning of faith. Biblical faith cannot be reduced to an intellectual matter, a belief that certain propositions are true. It is rather a living relationship which our beliefs are intended to express: a stance of counting on God, existing toward God and his kingdom. But what do we mean by God and his kingdom? Clearly not something that we understand or possess. God remains for us the infinite mystery, the goal and horizon of life, who never can be contained by our ideas, images or feelings. God is personal and free, and can only be known in the actual encounter with him.

In this sense, God and his kingdom, as revealed in Jesus, are always something new and surprising. The Christian is always faced with a new situation, for we are not yet in the kingdom, but are on our way. Faith is therefore a reality in process, oriented to the mysterious future in hope.

Superficially, the life of the individual Christian and of the church may seem to consist of repetition: of the same message, of the cycle of the liturgical year, of the whole content of Christian tradition passed from generation to generation. But in fact the life of faith is composed of unique and unrepeatable moments; no other can be the same as this moment in one's growth and encounter with God. And each moment is a new invitation. In our first reading the prophet Hosea speaks of God's intent for his people, portrayed as a wife who has grown tired of her husband: "I will lead her into the desert and speak to her heart; she shall respond there as in the days of her youth." However old and stale we may grow in our faith, God is ever courting us, calling us to new youth.

The church's cycles and seasons (like the coming season of Lent) are therefore not mere ritual repetitions, a kind of dramatic remembrance or playing out of the same events and ideas. Rather, they represent different aspects of a true call to an ever *new* conversion: a call from God to share his life, to turn around and reorient our lives to the mystery of love. It is not a matter of a seasonal "patching up" of the old relationship —there is no piecemeal approach to God: new cloth, new garments; we must be renewed as a whole.

The wine of the eucharist, the blood of Christ, is presented to us in each celebration as the sign of the "new" and eternal covenant. We must prepare ourselves to receive the new wine in new wineskins by becoming new selves.

Ninth Sunday of the Year

Dt 5:12–15
Ps 81:3–4, 5–6, 6–8, 10–11
2 Cor 4:6–11
Mk 2:23–3:6

The English poet and Jesuit Gerard Manley Hopkins re-counts how he once arrived at a hotel in France on a Sunday. The porter wished to carry his bags to his room, but Hopkins would not allow it, on the basis that for the porter to do it, as part of his job, would constitute servile work on the Lord's day. The porter's response was: *"Le bon Dieu n'est pas comme ça"*—"the good Lord is not like that."

It is of course not uncommon to find human scrupulosity and legalism projected onto God. Many people apparently never grow beyond the stage of seeing religion as a set of laws to be observed and tasks to be accomplished—so that it remains external, and never touches the core of the person.

In today's gospel, which contains two instances of conflict between Jesus and "the Pharisees"—a term used by Mark to represent the legalistic current in Judaism—we find a radical break with the immature notion of religion as law, and an affirmation of a relation with God based on human intelligence and responsibility.

In the first scene, concerning Jesus' disciples' transgression of the sabbath rest by plucking ears of grain, Jesus is portrayed as giving two very different reasons to justify their conduct. The first is in effect an appeal to common sense; in case of need, it is legitimate to break the letter of the law. Jesus argues like Hopkins' porter: God is not a legalist, and the law

49

does not envisage every circumstance. He appeals to the example of David, the king, to support his contention. Many of Jesus' contemporaries would be thoroughly in accord with this position. In fact, the saying "The sabbath was made for man, not man for the sabbath," appears to be a variant of a common rabbinic statement: "The sabbath is delivered unto you, and you are not delivered to the sabbath."

The following sentence, however, seems to place the matter in quite a different perspective: "So the Son of Man is Lord even of the sabbath." This statement follows logically from the preceding if the phrase "Son of Man" is taken simply to mean "man," in the sense of humanity, as it was commonly used in Aramaic. But most scholars believe that what is meant here is *the* Son of Man: the eschatological figure from the book of Daniel, represented as a glorified human being who would come at the end of time with the power of God's kingdom. This interpretation would accord with the use of "Lord" over the sabbath. But in this case Jesus seems to be appealing not to common sense in interpreting the law, but to his eschatological authority to supersede the law altogether. (It was on this basis, of course, that the early Christian community did in fact abandon the legal precepts of Judaism, including the observance of the sabbath day, which was replaced with the commemoration of the resurrection on Sunday.) It is hard to see how this second reason follows from the first; and many commentators believe that it is in fact an interpolation of the early community, interpreting Jesus' action, rather than a component of the original scene.

The second story also concerns the breaking of the sabbath rest, in this case for a healing. Here there is clearly more at issue than a liberal interpretation of the law. The rabbis admitted that it was legitimate and indeed a duty to work on the sabbath in order to save life, or in cases of urgency. But there is no apparent threat to life in the case of the man with the withered hand; a delay until the next day would not have been impossible. Jesus justified his action simply on the basis that he is doing good. The idea seems to be that there is always urgency in doing God's work of bringing the kingdom and battling against evil, of which sickness is a sign.

This gives an entirely new and more profound meaning to the idea that "the sabbath is made for man." The very purpose of the law is rethought. The sabbath is meant to honor and glorify God, but God's self-disclosure in Jesus reveals that God is honored and worshiped above all in the love of neighbor. God is revealed in Jesus as totally self-giving goodness. He is honored by the reception and sharing of that goodness in his creatures. "The good Lord is not like that"—not like a legalistic autocrat, not like a willful tyrant seeking to be obeyed, not like a supreme egotist wishing for adulation. What is he like? For Jesus, he is like a loving Father, who wishes above all the good of his children. As the second century father of the church, Irenaeus of Lyons, would later say: *Gloria Dei vivens homo*—"The glory of God is the living human being." This is not a reduction of God to a mere cipher for earthly human happiness, however; for the life and healing Jesus brings are directed precisely toward God and his kingdom, toward a being *for* God by being *for* others in a totally self-giving way. Thus Irenaeus adds to his famous statement: *vita autem hominis, visio Dei*—"and the life of humanity is the vision of God."

Tenth Sunday of the Year

Gen 3:9–15
Ps 130:1–2, 3–4, 5–6, 7–8
2 Cor 4:13–5:1
Mk 3:20–35

Most people are familiar with the "Star Wars" series of films and with J. R. R. Tolkien's classic fantasy *The Lord of the Rings*. These two trilogies, although vastly different in many ways, have one basic feature in common: both are mythical settings of the moral theme of the struggle of good against evil, portrayed as a battle of cosmic proportions.

There is also, of course, an explicitly religious version of the idea of the cosmic battle of the forces of good and evil. Its most classic form is in the religion of the Zoroastrians (today frequently called "Parsees"), the faith of ancient Persia (modern Iran). The Zoroastrian scriptures teach a system of dualism: that is, there is not one ultimate omnipotent being, but two competing forces: a totally good God and a totally evil spirit of destruction. These two from the beginning have been locked in mortal combat, and the earth has become the sphere of their struggle. In this way the Zoroastrians are able to explain the existence of evil in the world: God is totally good, as is everything he creates; evil comes about by the working of the evil spirit. God neither creates nor permits evil; he constantly struggles against it, and in the end, with the help of humanity, will be victorious.

The religion of ancient Persia made a number of significant contributions to the development of Judaism—in particu-

lar, the idea of the devil or the Satan, the spiritual adversary to
the salvation willed by God. The Jews already had a myth about
how evil came into the world: the story of the fall, which we
hear in the first reading. It is to be noted that in the original
story there is no hint of any spiritual being as the source of
temptation; the serpent of the story is merely one of the talking
(and walking!—according to the myth, the serpent does not
crawl until punished by God) animals of the garden. But by
shortly before the time of Jesus, many Jews had come to believe
in the angels and devils of Persian religion, and the tempter of
Genesis had been identified with the Satan, the adversary (cf.
Wis 2:24—"it was the devil's envy that brought death into the
world") making the Genesis story into a chapter in a larger
battle between God and the evil spirit.

The gospel presupposes this ongoing battle. Jesus proclaims and makes present God's kingdom, which means the
utter defeat of the powers of darkness. His healings and miracles are signs of that victory: health and human well-being are
what God desires and the demons oppose. It is for this reason,
Jesus argues in today's gospel, that his power cannot come
from demonic possession, but must be of God.

But the gospel is concerned with a further question, one
which must have been perplexing for the first generations of
Christians. Why was Jesus rejected by "his own"—by his
natural family, as well as by the majority of his people? As Mark
makes clear, Jesus' family thought that he was out of his mind
—and since the normal ancient Jewish explanation of mental
illness was demonic possession, this means they thought he was
possessed. Likewise, his opponents among the religious authorities make the same accusation. We who have long known
the story are quite used to the idea of Jesus' rejection; but it
must have been very difficult for early Christians to understand
how precisely those who were closest to him and had been

prepared by God's grace to receive his messiah were the ones who refused him and ultimately caused his death. Indeed, the idea is scandalous, and seems to bespeak a failure of God's plan. The answer which is given in the gospel to this problem is: sin. God's ultimate victory over the power of evil is assured, but humans must take sides in the struggle, and God does not remove our freedom. The ultimate sin—the only one which "cannot be forgiven"—is that of rejecting God's power working for the good, blaspheming against the Holy Spirit of God by identifying it with demonic madness.

It is also human freedom which determines fellowship with God and with Jesus. In the light of his rejection by "his own," Jesus proposes a new "family" based on doing the will of God. "Connections" do not count in God's kingdom: neither relationship to Jesus nor membership in the chosen people can suffice for salvation; one must choose personally to embrace the values which God proclaims and makes present in Jesus' teaching and work. The family of Jesus will be those who are in communion with God's struggle for the liberation of humanity from every power of evil and darkness.

Eleventh Sunday of the Year

Ez 17:22–24
Ps 92:2–3, 13–14, 15–16
2 Cor 5:6–10
Mk 4:26–34

Most of us have probably felt in some way the sentiments expressed in a song like "Sunrise, Sunset" from the musical "Fiddler on the Roof": parents wonder at how quickly the years have flown, how their children have grown. It seems only yesterday they were babies; suddenly, it seems, they are adults and living lives of their own. The opposite also happens: the parents whom we always thought of as young and strong and vital are suddenly old or infirm. Or we discover our own mortality and the loss of youth and possibilities; as one of the characters in Bergman's film "Fanny and Alexander" remarks, "First I'm a prince, the heir to the kingdom. Suddenly, before I know it, I am deposed; death taps me on the shoulder. . . ." Even in youth we have experienced the seemingly endless summer become as an instant, and we wonder where it went so quickly when we face the new school year in September.

In whatever context, we are all familiar with the sense of time flying: seeing something in its beginnings, and suddenly —so it seems—being confronted with a full-blown reality; the time in-between is not noticed.

Today's gospel evokes just such experiences, but without the sense of melancholy and loss that so frequently accompanies them. On the contrary, Jesus' parables speak of fully joyous events: the surprising abundance of nature, the miracle of growth. We wonder: Where did it come from? How could such small beginnings produce such results? The kingdom of God, Jesus tells us, is like this: the unspectacular, seemingly insignificant beginnings produce marvels.

Of course, growth does not happen all at once; wisdom does not come at once, nor age, nor maturity, nor love. But we most frequently do not notice the small daily increments; we are too close to them, and they are small enough to be within our ken; each single moment of growth is understandable and unsurprising—it is only at the end that we are amazed. The marvel actually happens beneath our eyes, but we do not see it as marvelous until we see the whole. It is not any particular moment, but the whole process which is astonishing. Each stage produces and explains the next; but the fact of there being growth at all—the fact that things can produce what is beyond themselves—produces wonder, and can only be seen as the gift of God.

The kingdom of God is also like this. It is the ordinary lives of people, lived in fidelity and unselfish love, often unnoticed or taken for granted, which become the marvel of God's triumphant presence in the world and bear fruit which is great and eternal. The final moment, the coming of the kingdom, has not yet happened, but it is right now underway. We come together in the eucharist to take note of it, to realize what we are about, and to renew our hope and dedication to what is slowly and secretly coming about in us by the power of God.

Our faith in this process, whose end we already anticipate with joy, also gives a new perspective to those many other instances of the flight of time which we experience. In the light of God's kingdom, they are not seen with melancholy as loss, but as growth toward that final stage in which the promise of each moment of life is fulfilled in the eternity of God.

Twelfth Sunday of the Year

Jb 38:1, 8–11
Ps 107:23–24, 25–26, 28–29, 30–31
2 Cor 5:14–17
Mk 4:35–41

An article that appeared recently in the news told of the extraordinary rescue of five Costa Rican fishermen on a thirty foot boat. Driven out to sea in a storm, they ran out of fuel trying to return to shore, and spent nearly five weeks adrift, at the mercy of the elements, on the Pacific Ocean, and were finally picked up off the coast of Hawaii. The captain was quoted as saying to their rescuers: "We never gave up hope because we have a great faith in God."

Anyone who has ever been in a storm at sea, or even seen a storm on the sea from the shore, can appreciate the drama of the story, and can relate to the words of the psalm:

> They who sailed the sea in ships . . .
> saw the works of the Lord,
> and his wonders in the abyss. . . .
> His command raised up a storm wind
> which tossed its waves on high.
> They mounted up to heaven; they sank to the depths;
> their hearts melted away in their plight.
> They cried to the Lord in their distress;
> from their straits he rescued them. . . .

We can also sympathize with the disciples in today's gospel passage, and feel the encouragement it gives in presenting the power of Jesus to save. But to understand more fully the meaning of this passage, we must place it in a larger context.

For the ancient Hebrews and other peoples of the near east, water was the primal element of chaos which God overcame and subdued in creating the world. He forms the earth by first binding and limiting the waters that surround it, fixing boundaries for the sea, which is still seen as the locus of evil and chaotic powers that can only be tamed by God. When God manifests his majesty and power to Job (first reading), he speaks of his shutting up the sea and setting its limits.

Against this background we hear the gospel story. Although the Sea of Galilee was frequently subject to sudden and violent storms, Jesus expresses his complete confidence in God by lying down to sleep. The disciples, however, show themselves to be of little faith; when the storm arises, they are terrified and call upon Jesus. Jesus' control of the wind and waves then shows him to be the Lord over the waters—that is, to have divine power—and the disciples are left in awe.

At first sight, Jesus' manifestation of power over the waters, though it recalls the majesty of God referred to in the first reading, seems to have an opposite message from that of the book of Job. God's discourse to Job is intended to silence the latter. When Job cries out in distress at his unjust suffering, God does not save him, nor does he answer his question; he merely shows his own power and absoluteness. The message of the book of Job is: this is God's world, and he is answerable to no one; his creatures must acknowledge and honor him for himself, not as someone who is useful to them. The world exists for God, not vice versa.

In the gospel, on the other hand, Jesus replies to the disciples' cry for help; his calming of the elements is not merely a manifestation of power, but a concrete instance of salvation. Yet the incident ends with the same reaction of awe that is Job's final response to God: the disciples find themselves in the presence of a power beyond that of the storm and the sea, and in some ways more terrifying. Jesus does indeed answer the prayer of the disciples, but he also rebukes them, telling them that their anxious prayer itself was a sign of lack of faith. He saves them, but he calls them to faith; he rescues them from the sea, but only in order to lead them to the cross.

The story does not merely tell us, then, that Jesus saves, but also intimates what salvation is: an abandonment of self to God and his love. It remains true for the Christian that it is God who is absolute; in loving and saving us, God can do no better or more for us than to bring us to himself. In the second reading, St. Paul says that Christ's salvific death occurred precisely so that we might live no longer for ourselves, but for him; to be saved means to be given a new center of life.

Anyone who has loved knows what it means to exist "for" another, rather than for oneself. Faith means recognizing and accepting that we exist for God; faith in Jesus means recognizing that God has come among us, so that to live for him means living for each other.

Thirteenth Sunday of the Year

Wis 1:13–15; 2:23–24
Ps 30:2, 4, 5–6, 11, 12, 13
2 Cor 8:7, 9, 13–15
Mk 5:21–43

For pious Muslims, one of the greatest of devotions is the meditation on the nature of God through the recitation of the "beautiful names" of Allah: the Beneficent, the Merciful, the Holy, the Mighty One, the All-Seeing, the Loving, and so forth. Among the great titles are *Al-Muhyî*, the Giver of Life, and *Al-Mumît*, the Creator of Death. Islam takes it for granted that all things—life and death, good and evil—come to us from God, who creates and controls everything according to his sovereign will. Such a view is not unknown to Jewish and Christian piety as well. Much of the Old Testament supports the idea of God as absolute Power, who sends both happiness and calamities; and it is certainly common to hear Christians speak of death and suffering as being controlled by God and given by his will.

Our first reading, however, implies a somewhat different perspective:

> God did not make death,
>   nor does he rejoice in the destruction of the living.
> For he fashioned all things that they might have being . . .
> by the envy of the devil, death entered the world,
>   and they who are in his possession experience it.

The book of Wisdom, the last of the Old Testament books to be written (probably less than a century before the birth of Christ), reflects ideas similar to those of the Zoroastrian religion of the Persian empire, to which the Jews had been subject in the period following the exile: God is totally good, and no evil comes from him; the world is his good creation; death and suffering are not part of his plan, but come from another power (the devil) who opposes God and seeks to corrupt his creatures. At its extreme, as in classical Zoroastrianism, this position becomes a real dualism: God is all-good, but he is not all-powerful; there is another eternal evil force against whom God as well as his creatures must struggle. Without adopting this extreme position, the Judaism represented by the author of Wisdom appropriated the crucial insight: God does not give death or suffering to humanity; they are the product of evil forces *against* God's will, and God seeks to overcome them.

Today's gospel passage exemplifies clearly the attitude of Jesus with regard to the ills that burden humanity. Without entering into speculation about the ultimate origins of evil or the metaphysics of God's omnipotence, the New Testament makes it clear that God, as manifest in Jesus, is on the side of life and healing; his power is at work to transform the world and overcome sorrow and death. Jesus' healings and miracles are the sign of God's will for the world's salvation. His proclamation that it is her faith which heals the afflicted woman indicates that for him faith is not a matter of fatalistic resignation or acceptance of evils as God's will, but precisely an attitude which confidently hopes for God's overcoming of evil.

Yet it is clear that the healings of Christ are not the ultimate word concerning salvation, but only an anticipation of it.

Even the little girl brought back from death would have to face an end to life at some time. It is in the resurrection of Jesus that we find God's final answer: not simply an aid to living or satisfaction of our needs, but the transformation of life itself and of its profoundest hopes.

Fourteenth Sunday of the Year

Ez 2:2–5
Ps 123:1–2, 2, 3–4
2 Cor 12:7–10
Mk 6:1–6

Probably the most fundamental attribute of God in religious consciousness—what makes him divine—is his power. According to many scholars, the ability to respond to human needs is crucial to a truly living and religious concept of God as one who is worshiped—as opposed to a merely theoretical and philosophical idea of a supreme being. Those prayers in the eucharist derived from the Roman liturgical tradition (many of our opening prayers, for example) clearly reflect such an attitude; the typical form of address is "Almighty and eternal God . . ."

Such a conception of God—as the almighty power— probably corresponds to most Christians' most basic, even if unreflective, religious instincts. Our prayer in general is not simple meditation, like that of the Buddhist, nor disinterested and one-sided glorification of God, like that of the Muslim; we expect God to hear us, and to respond. Scripture scholars tell us, indeed, that this is the primary characteristic of the God of the Bible: he is a God who *acts* for his people. The psalm we recite today is an eloquent example of this dialogical kind of relationship and expectation: "Our eyes are fixed on the Lord, pleading for his mercy."

It is all the more perplexing, then, when God's power seems to fail us, despite our pleading in faithfulness and hope. St. Paul's confession in the second reading, inspiring as it may be, is nevertheless somewhat unsettling when we reflect on exactly what he is saying: he has begged for help, and God's response is that his power will be shown in *not* answering Paul's ardent plea. Somehow, paradoxically, Paul's weakness and distress are to be the sign of God's power at work in him.

The limitation of the working of God's power figures also in the gospel. Mark tells us bluntly that Jesus was *unable* to work any miracles in his own country (it is notable that Matthew, in the parallel passage, softens the statement, saying only that Jesus *did not* work miracles there; but the "could not" [*ouk edunato*] of Mark is unambiguous). Furthermore, the whole passage is concerned with an even more striking apparent failure: for here is the messiah, the one longed and prayed for; and his presence is not recognized, his message does not succeed, even among his own kindred and neighbors! Can this be the answer of the "all-mighty" to the supplications and hopes of his people?

But the gospel also gives us another perspective on the matter. We are told that Jesus was amazed at the lack of faith that he encountered (*ethaumazen dia ten apistian auton:* "he was astonished by their lack of faith," rather than the freer "so much did their lack of faith distress him" of the lectionary translation). If we are surprised and distressed by the failures of God's power to change the world, God (to speak anthropomorphically) must be even more so. The hardness and blindness of human hearts, to which the scriptures ascribe the rejection of Jesus and his ultimate submission to death, cannot but appear both incredibly absurd and unbearably pathetic to the point of view of absolute love for us.

This is not to say that if we had faith, God's power would be freed and all our requests would be answered. The example of St. Paul and of Jesus himself should prevent us from drawing such a naive conclusion. But the fate of Jesus—which we celebrate in each eucharist—shows us how we are to reevaluate our ideas of power itself and of its purpose. If we have faith, that power *is* freed: not simply to serve our present wants, but to be power *over us*, to transform us, and to make us see that what we truly and most deeply need and desire is precisely to be for God and for each other.

Fifteenth Sunday of the Year

Am 7:12-15
Ps 85:9-10, 11-12, 13-14
Eph 1:3-14
Mk 6:7-13

A few years ago I took part in a conference for teachers of philosophy in seminaries and theological schools, both Roman Catholic and Protestant. The universal sentiment among the participants was that theological students did not have enough philosophical background for their theological studies, but it soon became apparent that there was a vast difference in the context of the complaint. One Roman Catholic professor was lamenting that philosophy requirements have dropped so radically in seminaries that students now can begin graduate studies in theology after having had only fifteen credits of philosophy. "Fifteen credits!" exclaimed an Evangelical Protestant in the group. "We'd be delighted if our students had fifteen credits of philosophy. You have to realize that in our church, the difficulty is getting ministers to go to seminary at all."

I know from numerous conversations, as well as from surveys that have been done, that many Catholics think that their priests are often poorly prepared for ministry. Nevertheless, they would probably be aghast at the idea of eliminating seminary training and allowing anyone who felt a calling simply to open up a church and start preaching—as is the case in some Protestant denominations. Most of us probably take it for granted that better ministry calls for an increase in education and training, for more professionalism and qualifications, not less.

In this perspective, today's readings may give us pause. The first lesson recounts how the prophet Amos (eighth century B.C.) was confronted by the political/religious authorities because of his strident denunciations of the moral and religious situation in Israel. The priest Amaziah, speaking on behalf of the king, commands Amos to depart, contemptuously calling him a "visionary," and telling him to earn his living by prophesying elsewhere. He presumes that Amos is a professional prophet like many others of the times who, for a fee, acted as seers and oracles. Amos gives the startling reply that he is no professional; he is a simple shepherd, with no training or affiliation; he prophesies not out of choice or for gain, but because he was called by God to do so. If we read the book of Amos, with its forceful and heartfelt teaching on social justice and true fidelity to God, we cannot but feel that there is a credibility to his claim which contrasts not only with the semi-pagan professional prophets, but also with the official priest of the institutional religion.

In our gospel passage, we hear of the first mission of the disciples of Jesus. Like Amos, they were taken from their ordinary and humble occupations and sent to preach with urgency. Their only preparation was their life with Jesus—who was himself no religious professional, not a priest or official, a man with no institutional standing and (so far as we know) no special training.

All of this is certainly not to imply that we might be better off trusting to God's raising up charismatic leaders for the church rather than relying on institutional ministry. But it does remind us that training and professionalism and institutional standing cannot substitute for what is essential in Christian ministry: the internal experience of conversion, the enthusiasm, conviction and dynamism that stem from a personal encounter with God. We cannot expect these to be provided by education or professional competence. In the last analysis, ministry is not a "job" in the sense of a task to be performed in order to make a living; it must be life itself. And for this same reason it cannot be a "job" in the sense of a specialty confined to some members of the community. There are, of course, specialized ministers in the church, with a need for particular training and competence. May they increase, and their preparation be more demanding! But what is crucial to their vocation can only come about in them in the context of a whole community which realizes that, as St. Paul writes, "in Christ *you too were chosen.*"

We have all been "sealed with the Holy Spirit" which gives the experience of God and the dynamism to bring his love to the world. When ministers come out of and go into such a community of ministry, then the contrast of charism and institution disappears in collaboration. "God has given *us* the wisdom to understand fully the mystery, the plan he was pleased to decree in Christ . . . to bring all things in the heavens and on earth into one under Christ's headship."

Sixteenth Sunday of the Year

Jer 23:1–6
Ps 23:1–3, 3–4, 5, 6
Eph 2:13–18
Mk 6:30–34

In Isak Dinesen's short story "Tales of Two Gentlemen," an elderly Italian recalls the theological musings of his grandfather, who was a sheep farmer:

> "We suffer much. We go through many dark hours of doubt, dread and despair, because we cannot reconcile our idea of divinity with the state of things in the universe round us. I myself as a young man brooded a good deal over the problem. Later on I arrived at the conviction that we should, more easily and more thoroughly than we now do or ever have done, understand the nature and laws of the Cosmos if we would from the beginning recognize its originator and upholder as being of the female sex.
>
> "We speak about Providence and announce: The Lord is my shepherd, He will provide. But in our hearts we know that we should demand from our own shepherds ... a providential care of our sheep very different from the one to which we are ourselves submitted, and which appears mainly to provide us with blood and tears.
>
> "But say instead, of Providence: 'She is my shepherdess'—and you will at once realize in what way you may expect to be provided for.
>
> "For to a shepherdess tears are convenient and precious, like rain ... like pearls, or like falling stars.... And as to the shedding of blood, this to our shepherdess—as to any lady—is a high privilege and is inseparably united with

the sublimest moments of existence, with promotion and beatification. What little girl will not joyously shed her blood in order to become a virgin, what bride not hers in order to become a wife, what young wife not hers to become a mother?

"Man, troubled and perplexed about the relation between divinity and humanity, is ever striving to find a foothold in the matter by drawing on his own normal experience. He will view it in the light of relations between tutor and pupil, or of commander and soldier, and he will lose breath—and heart—in search and investigation. The ladies, whose nature is nearer to the nature of the deity, take no such trouble; they see the relation between the Cosmos and the Creator quite plainly as a love affair. . . ."

(from *Last Tales*)

It is certainly true that the image of God as our shepherd becomes problematic if we interpret it in terms of his running the world and keeping us, his sheep, from harm. It is possibly also true that a certain male bias exerts an influence in our imagining God's relation to the world as one of control and domination rather than one of love and invitation, and may lead us to harbor false expectations.

Of course, it is understandable that we should appeal to God, in his power and goodness, in the face of human power so frequently aligned with evil. In today's first reading, the prophet Jeremiah declaims against the bad shepherds of God's people. (It should be borne in mind that while the image of "shepherd" has for us a religious and even clerical association —we even refer to "pastors" of churches—in the Old Testament it refers above all to the *rulers* of the land, whose function encompassed both religious and secular spheres. Abraham, Moses, and David were all shepherds, and it was above all the king who was endowed with their mantle of leadership.) The prophet's diatribe concludes with the promise that God himself will provide a righteous king to shepherd his people. (The symbolic name of this future monarch, "Yahweh is our justice" [Yhwh ṣidqēnû], is in fact a reversal of the name of the then-reigning and rejected king, Zedekiah [ṣidqî-yāhû, "my justice is Yahweh"].) The true successor to David, the king and shepherd, the anointed messiah, will bring about God's own kingdom.

For the Christian, this prophecy is fulfilled in the person of Jesus, and the juxtaposition of the Old Testament and gospel readings in this liturgy is intended to underscore the fact. Yet the identification of God's good shepherd with Jesus does not change our fundamental situation: the statement "The Lord is my shepherd" still does not describe how the world is run or what security we can expect from life. In fact, Jesus refuses to be the shepherd-king. Whatever may be the more precise meaning of the so-called "messianic secret" in Mark's gospel, it is in any case clear that Jesus rejects the messiahship in its popular political understanding. When he has pity on the people because he finds them like sheep without a shepherd, his reaction is not to rule, but to teach.

While Jesus preaches the coming of God's kingdom, his peace and love reigning over humanity, his life does not provide a triumph over the forces of evil to establish that kingdom; and his followers, far from being assured of success and happiness in the world, are invited to follow in his footsteps to the cross. The way of salvation still demands blood and tears and self-sacrifice; the relation of God to the world is still, as Dinesen's character puts it, more like a love affair than like a well-run flock.

And this is as it must be, for God comes to us in our freedom and our humanity, and does not force our submission or take away the risk-filled world that makes our freedom possible. What we mean when we claim God as our shepherd is our unshakable confidence that he is near and that he provides; even in the valley of the shadow of death, he is with us. But what the image of the pasture and banquet points to is the food for a human spirit; and that food is the knowledge of God and his love as being ever faithful and unfailing, and as being our true destiny. When we can accept this deeply in our hearts, then it becomes true: with God as my shepherd, there is nothing I shall want; for having God, we have all.

Seventeenth Sunday of the Year

2 Kgs 4:42–44
Ps 145:10–11, 15–16, 17–18
Eph 4:1–6
Jn 6:1–15

Many families are probably like my own in using the summer as a time for gatherings. It is a season of picnics and gatherings and dinner parties. One of the results of all the socializing and hospitality is that the refrigerator seems always to end up full of left-overs. This can be either a pleasant or an unpleasant fact of summer life, depending upon one's taste, and most people probably have to cope with it. It may come as a surprise, however, to hear that left-overs have a theological significance.

Both the first reading and the gospel of today's liturgy place great emphasis on the fact that there is food left over. It is a sign of the abundance of the feeding; there is more than enough. This underscores the fact that it is God who provides the food, and it makes the meal into a sign of his kingdom.

For us, of course, abundance is a part of the normal situation of life; we are used to left-overs. Even on the large scale, our society over-produces. Our country not only normally has huge stockpiles of surplus foodstuffs, but we even pay farmers not to produce certain crops, for fear of a glut on the market. Our situation, however, is extremely abnormal. Most of humanity through most of history—including today, in much of the world—has lived at a bare subsistence level: there was rarely enough to eat to satisfaction, let alone to have left over. Food was scarce, and life was precarious.

For this reason, food in abundance was significant, and meant abundant life; it symbolized the gift of God par excellence. To have more than what was needed, to have extra, was a grace, a gift of overwhelming generosity. In this context, abundance could be seen as the sign of the joy of God's kingdom. In the gospel, Jesus is recognized because of his performance of this sign of feeding. "This is undoubtedly the prophet who is to come into the world"—that is, the "prophet like Moses," who was expected to come in messianic times. Moses had given the people "bread from heaven" in the form of manna in the wilderness; the prophet of the last days would also bring food from God, a sign of the eschatological banquet to come.

Naturally, the readings are also intended to point to the celebration of the eucharist, the new "bread from heaven" and the sign of the fellowship and banquet of the kingdom. At one time the eucharist was seen principally in terms of the "real presence" of Christ. The symbolism of food was largely forgotten, or was deemphasized almost to the point of denial. People were told not to chew the host; the wafers were made to be white, flat, and uniform, often with pictures engraved upon them—as unlike ordinary bread as possible. The time of communion was seen as a special moment of presence of Jesus, and therefore a time of intimate prayer in silence. The recovery of the sense of a communal meal does not reduce the mystery of the eucharist, but attempts to extend that mystery to the rest of life: not only this special moment of worship, but all life is engaged in the mystery of God. It is not a question of reducing the eucharist to symbolic food, but of raising food to a symbol of God.

This symbol bespeaks not only God's presence in Jesus and his community, but also God's action. We celebrate the fact that God feeds us, cares for us; that he not only meets our needs, but allows us to taste the abundance of the kingdom, the graciousness of his gift. The joy which the eucharist conveys through the recognition of God's grace is meant to lead us to the insight that existence itself is a gift and a continual act of God—a gift which is not merely physical survival, but super-abundant being, the call to share the life of God in love.

Eighteenth Sunday of the Year

Ex 16:2–4, 12–15
Ps 78:3–4, 23–24, 25, 54
Eph 4:17, 20–24
Jn 6:24–35

Any student of the English language quickly comes to appreciate that its vast powers of expression come from the confluence of the diverse linguistic streams that have flowed into it during its long history. In some cases we have two sets of words for the same things: one set coming from Latin, through French, and the other from Germanic roots through Anglo-Saxon. Frequently the synonymous words are used in different circumstances, reflecting the social history at the time of the language's formation. So, for example, animals on the hoof are generally called by their Anglo-Saxon names, while the same animals cooked and served have names from the French-speaking upper classes. Thus we have a calf on the farm, but veal on the table; likewise with cattle and beef, swine and pork, sheep and mutton. (One remarkable effect of this is that English speakers are able to eat and talk about many foods without ever thinking of the animals they come from.)

Something of the same phenomenon occurs with our religious language. It tends for historical reasons to be Latin-derived, and its terms frequently occur almost exclusively in religious contexts, separate from everyday usage. This fact may cut us off from recognizing some of the dimensions of the meaning of what we are saying. For example: we may speak of Jesus with two Latin derived words as our "spiritual nourishment." If we tried to translate this phrase into plain Anglo-Saxon words, one way of putting it might be: Jesus is "food for thought"—for the word "spiritual" refers to the faculty that makes us human, that is, the faculty of thinking, being conscious, reasoning and willing.

This is in fact the first meaning of the idea of "nourishment" by Christ: a change in our minds, in our way of thinking. St. Paul says in today's second reading: "You must no longer live as the pagans do—their minds empty"; you must "acquire a fresh, spiritual way of thinking." And in today's gospel, the beginning of the Johannine discourse on the bread of life, Jesus presents himself as nourishment for the mind, as wisdom. The context of Jesus' language is drawn from Proverbs, 9:1ff: "Wisdom . . . has dispatched her maidservants and proclaimed from the city's heights . . . 'Come and eat my bread, drink the wine I have prepared!' " It also plainly recalls the book of Sirach (24:21f), in which Wisdom says: "They who eat me will hunger for more, they who drink me will thirst for more." Jesus however is the perfect wisdom which satisfies our spiritual hunger and thirst completely.

The dialogue of Jesus with the crowd reveals their misunderstanding of him; they keep reducing to a material level his effort to bring them to a spiritual way of thinking. They desire material bread produced by a miracle, while Jesus wishes to give them wisdom; they do not understand that the feeding with bread is a sign of what must happen to their minds.

It is easy for us as well to separate religion from our minds, to relegate it to a "mystical" supernatural realm which has no connection with thinking or acting humanly in the world. But Christian religion is explicitly an address to our mind: not merely a mystical communion, but a real unity based on seeing a common meaning in life, having the same food for thought embodied in the food we share in sacrament. It is also a call for us to be the same kind of nourishment for each other: our lives should be such that they lead others not to having empty minds, but to seeking meaning in life because they see in us minds filled with wisdom and ultimate value.

Nineteenth Sunday of the Year

1 Kgs 19:4–8
Ps 34:2–3, 4–5, 6–7, 8–9
Eph 4:30–5:2
Jn 6:41–51

It is one of the signs of the increased health consciousness of the American people that we now find on our supermarket shelves an abundance of healthy bread. Where once was seen nothing but soft, pulpy, bleached white and uniformly pre-sliced loaves, where even the occasional whole wheat loaf seemed a grudging concession to fanatics, now one can select from a dazzling variety of breads of many grains, of a myriad of shapes and consistencies. Good bread has become the symbol of the good life. It stands appropriately for our concern for health and well-being, since bread has always in western culture been the symbol of survival itself: the staff of life.

In biblical imagery, as we saw already in last Sunday's readings, bread is also the symbol of spiritual life. In the book of Sirach (15:3), we read that Wisdom "will nourish him [who fears the Lord] with the bread of understanding and will give him the water of learning to drink." Understanding and learning are seen as the food and drink of the mind, its source of vitality.

The image is a powerful one to reflect upon. What is it, after all, that nourishes us spiritually? What gives us strength of spirit, satisfaction of mind, well-being, courage, and the ability to go on? What is our real bread? What the Old Testament refers to as learning and understanding should not be taken in a purely intellectualist sense: they refer to living knowledge of

God and of his will. In our more psychologically introspective modern context, we might say that what gives us spiritual health is "meaning" in life: the knowledge of a purpose and goal in life; self-confidence and hope; the affirmation of our being and our value—that is, love.

There are, of course, other things which people use to feed their minds and hearts. One may try to make life meaningful by self-assertion, egotism, domination over others; by possessiveness, grasping at objects or experiences; by fantasy and illusion. But every attempt to substitute self-made meaning for love, hope, and knowledge, while it may produce momentary satisfaction, will ultimately fail to nourish. Only from God can we receive the absolute affirmation of our being, in spite of sin and the certitude of death. Only "bread from heaven" can satisfy our hunger for spiritual food and give us the ability to go on.

Jesus claims to be this bread from heaven: the wisdom from God which affirms our being and nourishes our spirit. But an objection is raised: How can he be "from heaven"— how can he be *God's* giving of meaning to life—if he is a human being whose origins and family are well known? (Note that the objection at this point in the discourse is not that Jesus is "bread," but that he is "from heaven"; only later comes the scandal at the idea of eating his flesh). Jesus' reply is that he is "from God," precisely in his humanity.

This faces us squarely with the central idea of the incarnation. Jesus' being from God does not depend upon his descending from heaven in a miraculous manner, as the objectors suppose; it is not his physical origin which determines his sonship from God, any more than it is physical food which he offers. Being from God means having "seen" the Father—that is, having the interior experience of God, and coming into being on the level of human spirit because of that experience.

Only those can accept Jesus as heavenly bread, as nourishment for the spirit, who have also had something of the same experience: "No one can come to me unless the Father who sent me draws him." This is the reality of being "taught" directly by God to which Jesus refers. Those who have had this experience can recognize God's word and wisdom when it appears among them; they can be "nourished" by Jesus as the concrete assurance of God's gift of life.

Twentieth Sunday of the Year

Prv 9:1–6
Ps 34:2–3, 10–11, 12–13, 14–15
Eph 5:15–20
Jn 6:51–58

In a passage in Flannery O'Connor's short novel *The Violent Bear It Away* an eccentric old man catechizes a young boy, his great-nephew:

> "You were born into bondage and baptized into freedom, into the death of the Lord, into the death of the Lord Jesus Christ."
>
> Then the child would feel a sullenness creeping over him, a slow warm rising resentment that this freedom had to be connected with Jesus and that Jesus had to be the Lord.
>
> "Jesus is the bread of life," the old man said.
>
> The boy, disconcerted, would look off into the distance over the dark blue treeline where the world stretched out, hidden and at its ease. In the darkest, most private part of his soul, hanging upside down like a sleeping bat, was the certain, undeniable knowledge that he was not hungry for the bread of life. . . .
>
> The boy sensed that this was the heart of his great-uncle's madness, this hunger, and what he was secretly afraid of was that it might be passed down, might be hidden in the blood and might strike some day in him and then he would be torn by hunger like the old man, the bottom split out of his stomach so that nothing would heal or fill it but the bread of life.

The church speaks a great deal about Jesus as the bread of life; the eucharist is its principal symbol. But many people, like the boy in Flannery O'Connor's story, are not hungry for the bread of life—although some of them may nevertheless make a point of being Christians and participating in the church's rituals for quite different reasons, not altogether admitted into consciousness.

What does it mean for Jesus to be the bread from heaven —or, as he puts it more graphically in today's gospel, for him to give his flesh to be eaten? The readings of the past two Sundays, from the first part of John's discourse on the bread of life, have a clear reference to the theme of Wisdom (as also in today's first reading): the "bread" which Jesus gives is his teaching. But today's passage goes farther. John portrays a scene in which Jesus' words create scandal and commotion among his hearers: in terms which obviously refer to the Christian eucharist, he insists that the true nourishment from God means eating *him*.

The offensiveness of such an idea to a Jewish audience would be easily understandable—and indeed foreshadows the difficulty of accepting the eucharist for many others as well. The phrase "to eat someone's flesh" for the Jews connoted a hostile act. The drinking of blood of any kind was forbidden by the law; the notion of drinking human blood would be doubly appalling.

Taken together, however, the words "flesh and blood" signify the whole life of a creature, its entirety. The phrase is especially connected with the giving and taking of life in sacrifice, as in the temple worship. It is this connection which explains the meaning of this passage for Christians, to whom it is of course addressed. To eat Jesus' flesh and drink his blood is to be nourished by his sacrificial death: that is, to find our real life in living a similar life and dying a similar death in self-offering to the Father. It is not merely a matter of receiving Jesus' doctrine, but of sharing his life and fate. As the philosopher Alfred North Whitehead wrote, the Buddha gave his doctrine for the world; Christ gave his life. It is Jesus' very life which must nourish us by our partaking it, internalizing it, making it our food.

Eating this food means "remaining in" Jesus, and having life "because of" him, as he has life because of the Father. It means that we find our true existence not in living "for" ourselves, but, as the fourth eucharistic prayer says, in living "for" God; it is the sacramental expression of the seeming paradox reiterated several times in the synoptics: he who would save his life must lose it.

It is emphasized by John that Jesus' flesh and blood are "real" or "true" food and drink: that is, those which satisfy not merely physical hunger, but the hunger for genuine life, the life we share with God, both now and eternally. What Jesus claims to nourish is not merely our animal existence, but the truest kind of human life: the kind which is like God's life, lived in total love. This is the true challenge of the eucharist: to desire to be fed toward love, toward being for others. In each of us there is the spark of ego, of narrowness, of resentment, as in Flannery O'Connor's boy, that life must be connected with Jesus; there is something that is not hungry for the bread of life. But insofar as we have been loved and have loved, we have experienced already what true life is about, and can only be satisfied with this true bread that leads to life which is eternally valid.

Twenty-First Sunday of the Year

Jos 24:1–2, 15–17, 18
Ps 34:2–3, 16–17, 18–19, 20–21, 22–23
Eph 5:21–32
Jn 6:60–69

There is scarcely a name in the Roman Catholic world which would be less likely to be associated with criticism of the institutional church—much less with entertaining the idea of leaving it—than that of Joseph Cardinal Ratzinger, the prefect of the Congregation of the Doctrine of the Faith. Yet at an earlier point in his career, when he was still a professor of theology, he was the co-author of a small book dealing with exactly those themes. The first section of the book was entitled, "Why I Am Still a Christian." Ratzinger's contribution, which followed, was an essay on "Why I Am Still in the Church."

The essence of Ratzinger's answer to this question comes down to a paraphrase of Peter's answer when Jesus asks the twelve whether they will leave him also: "Where else shall we go?" We do not belong to the church, according to Professor Ratzinger, because it is perfect, or because it has all the answers, or because it is always comforting to belong to it, but because, despite its many flaws, we find in it something which is crucial and indispensable. Remaining in the church, then, is a challenge: to be faithful to that truth which is its essence, while transcending its limitations and faults.

A good example presents itself in the material of today's second reading. Paul says in the letter to the Ephesians: "Wives, obey your husbands in everything," and, at the end of the reading, the lector proclaims, "This is the word of the Lord." Many modern women find it offensive that a patriarchal structure—granted that it was the norm in St. Paul's social context—should be implicitly affirmed as being of divine institution. Of course, it would be fundamentalist to assume that everything asserted in the Bible has divine authority, or that liturgical usage excuses us from the task of interpretation and understanding. Clearly, in this case Paul has taken for granted the anthropology of his times and background, with the social structure it implied. He presumes that people are not all on the same level; that there is a hierarchy of being and of function, in which the male has a "higher" role, similar to that of Christ with regard to the church. Yet what is crucial in the passage is that even in accepting and consecrating male authority, Paul introduces a principle which radically transforms it; for he makes its model the behavior of Christ. Husbands are to love their wives in the way Christ loves the church—i.e. in a self-sacrificing way, in which headship is not a matter of lording it over others, but of service. Indeed, husband and wife are meant to be "one," as Christ is with the church. All of this means that Paul is in an essential way beyond his times with regard to the status of women, precisely because, although he accepts as "natural" the higher status of the male, he also sees all natural human relationship as radically transformed by the new principle of the love of Christ. (This is seen not only in the case of male/female, but also in the essential equality of slave and free, Jew and Gentile, which Paul elsewhere cites as parallels.)

Nevertheless, it remains true that Paul accepts role models in marriage which are not eternally fixed, and it is necessary for us to separate the "essence" of his Christian message from the assumed (although also transformed) cultural context in which he presents it. Faithfulness to the essential message may force us to go beyond Paul's context in ways which would have been unimaginable to him (so, for example, the current marriage rite explicitly proclaims that both partners are equals).

Such examples point to the complexity of the challenge of deciding to be a Christian or to belong to the church. In today's first reading, Joshua presents the Israelites with the option of serving the God who led them from Egypt or falling away to serve the pagan gods; Jesus' disciples are likewise faced with the choice of opting to follow him or to leave. And of course, at a deep level, each of us must make such a fundamental decision: for or against God, for or against Jesus. But the option is rarely presented in such clearly defined terms. For God and Jesus are mediated to us through other human beings; and the presence of the absolute, the divine, may be obscured by the historical and social limitations of its mediators—as in the case of St. Paul on the place of women—or, more seriously, by their moral failures and intellectual blindness. In today's gospel it is the difficulty of Jesus' message of self-sacrifice (being nourished by his flesh and blood, i.e. by his sacrificial death) which is a scandal to the disciples; but there is another level of scandal when it is not the message, but the lives and limitations of its bearers which become the difficulty.

For many modern people, the question about remaining in the church has become a particularly vital one, for their objection is not to Jesus, but to the community that claims to represent him. At one time, for most westerners believing in God, being a Christian and belonging to the church all seemed synonymous. Where else could one go? There simply was no other accessible mediation of sacred experience. This situation no doubt frequently led to a kind of spiritual inertia, in which belonging to the church was taken for granted and no decision at all was required; personal commitment was minimal, and the religious question could fade into the background of existence.

But in the modern global village, with widespread education and the public secularization of society, alternatives abound; and precisely for this reason, the question of commitment becomes urgent. People no longer ask, "Where else can we go?" There are other ways to God than through Christ; other ways to Christ than through Christianity; other ways of being Christian than the institutional church; indeed, other values than the sacred to compete for our attention.

Remaining in the church, then, is a decision that cannot be taken for granted. Each of us must ask ourselves, like Ratzinger, "Why am I still in the church?" Seeing the flaws in the church, far from being disloyal, is critical to our finding what is truly essential to our belonging. Even more essential is recognizing the challenge of Jesus and his message. Many people today see clearly that the values of the gospel are not in accord with the "lifestyle" they would like to lead, and leave the church—sometimes with regret—rather than be dishonest. All the gospels tell us that Jesus was abandoned by many of his disciples. Jesus' life and message are not innocuous; if we do not find them challenging, perhaps we have not really heard their demand. If we choose with eyes open and in honesty to belong to a community which strives, imperfectly, to fulfill such a demanding mission as selflessness and universal love and communion, it can only be because we see that we really have nowhere else to go; because for all the difficulty of the cross and the scandal of a human church, we are convinced that here we find the words of eternal life.

Twenty-Second Sunday of the Year

Dt 4:1–2, 6–8
Ps 15:2–3, 3–4, 4–5
Jas 1:17–18, 21–22, 27
Mk 7:1–8, 14–15, 21–23

We have all heard the expression, "Cleanliness is next to godliness" (to which some wags add, "and if you can't be godly, at least be clean"). We have also probably all met some people who are preoccupied with cleanliness to an extreme degree, so that it becomes an obsession. Sometimes this kind of fixation can actually be a sign of neurosis, as in the case of people who continually feel the need to wash their hands, dozens of times a day, despite the fact that there is no apparent reason for it. Compulsive hand-washing is of course a symbolic act: it represents the person's desire to be rid of some deep mental preoccupation. The "dirt" to be gotten rid of is something perceived as threatening that preys upon the mind and causes anxiety. The process of washing expresses the desire to be safe, to escape from the "dirt," to do something concrete about the imagined threat. The person does not face this on a conscious level, of course, but the unconscious preoccupation expresses itself externally in an uncontrollable urge to attain cleanliness, purity and thus safety. This is a dramatic symptom, but many small and almost unnoticed forms of compulsive behavior may likewise be unconscious efforts to deal with worrisome psychological tension in a ritualized way. There are probably few people who on a conscious or unconscious level have not had to deal with a sense of anxiety or dread.

This object of dread may be experienced in various ways,

but the ultimate source of all anxiety is the uncertainty of life itself, its threatened character: our unsureness of our own worth and value; the fear of rejection, failure, death, nothingness, meaninglessness.

Religion is about precisely these fears; it is supposed to bring us face to face with them, to confront life in its ultimate perspective and seek an ultimate answer. But sometimes religion does the opposite, and becomes a form of behavior parallel to neurosis: it does not face the great issues, but avoids them, and gives people instead a series of ritual actions which are intended to give them a sense of safety and escape.

The gospel criticizes this tendency in the religion of the Pharisees, which expressed a kind of communal anxiety in its insistence on correct ritual and exact keeping of the law. The law was seen as God's way of life. But how could one be sure of keeping it correctly, of doing everything properly, of fulfilling all the demands? In Pharisaic Judaism, an oral code arose to explain and expand the law, telling one exactly what to do in order to be sure of keeping it: a tradition of rituals to encompass all of life and keep one safe.

For Jesus, this kind of religion misses the point. True religion is about the heart, not about external rituals and observances; it concerns what comes from within. How do we know that we are doing right, that we are fulfilling what God "wants"? How can we be safe? How can we avoid the awesome and perhaps frightening feeling of answerability for life? We cannot. We are free, we are responsible, and we are at risk. But God is not looking to "catch" us. The message of the gospel is good news. We are to dismiss our anxiety at its very source— not by avoiding risk or evading the deep moral choices that face us and seeking safety in external forms of ritual religion, but by facing the awe-inspiring reality: God loves us; the ultimate reality is with us, and calls us out of ourselves to him.

Twenty-Third Sunday of the Year

Is 35:4–7
Ps 146:7, 8–9, 9–10
Jas 2:1–5
Mk 7:31–37

In the play "Children of a Lesser God"—made more recently into a film—we are confronted dramatically and forcefully with the problems faced by a teacher of the deaf and dumb, and the difficulties he finds in establishing real communication, especially with the best and most sensitive of his students. The story had a particular impact on me because it dramatized and illustrated stories that I had heard from a friend whose life work is with deaf children. But while the film had a happy outcome, and gave an impression of how rewarding such work can be when it meets with success, the real-life situation frequently shows more the side of frustration and pathos. Deaf children face a terrible handicap in learning; they remain years behind other children, even if they have great native intelligence. They frequently are unable to get beyond an elementary level, not only in learning but also in emotional development. Often they cannot communicate even with their own families.

In her last years, my grandmother was blind, and I frequently reflected on what a terrible deprivation the lack of sight is. But experts say that the lack of hearing is an even worse handicap. Hearing and speaking are what open us to each other and to the human world. They make us capable of dialogue, both in the literal sense and in the extended sense that follows from it: relationship. Without these, we would remain totally closed in upon ourselves; we would be observers of the world, but not real participants.

Recalling these things will perhaps help us to appreciate what today's gospel is about. The physical miracle is of course to be understood as fulfilling the prophecy of Isaiah which we hear in the first reading and as signifying the coming of God's kingdom of healing and peace. But Mark also intends the "opening" of ears and mouth by Jesus to be symbolic: it is not simply what happens to the man in the story, but what happens spiritually to every Christian. From very early times the church adopted this passage for use in the baptismal ceremony, in which it survives as an optional rite even today: the priest touches the ears and mouth of the baptized and prays that they be opened to God's word.

To be able to hear and to speak is to be capable of dialogue. For Mark, this is not restricted to the human level, but also (metaphorically) applies to communication with God. Christ gives us the capacity for dialogue with the Father.

Our familiarity with such ideas should not prevent us from realizing that this is a remarkable claim. What can dialogue with God mean? How can one "hear" or "speak" on a spiritual level? Clearly, if we take seriously the idea of an immaterial and all-knowing God, there can be no question of an actual interchange of words or ideas between us and the divinity. Nevertheless, we claim that something analogous to speech and hearing occurs. What, then, is the essence of these human functions?

Dialogue is first of all a matter of interpellation: one is addressed by another; there is a personal "call," an imperative to attend to the other as a person, not as a thing; the other becomes for us not merely a function of our own existence, or an object in the horizon of our minds, but another "self" over against our own.

Dialogue also involves an invitation to trust; saying something implies a claim to communicate the truth, and asks the hearer to put faith in the one who speaks. Speech also communicates information, and thus contributes to the other's being and growth. Finally, speaking and hearing are aimed at a communion of life, at some level. When we share something of our mind, we are giving of ourselves to another. Dialogue is thus an event of purposely and freely uniting separate persons, and is therefore an act of love (albeit with many very different levels of profundity).

The gospel indicates in symbol that Christ makes it possible for such things—"hearing" and "speaking"—to happen in our relation with God: direct relation, dialogue, like that which occurs in face to face communication with another person. We are able to give our minds and hearts to God, and to share in his mind and heart.

How does Christ open our ears and mouth? How do we become capable of sharing the mind and heart of God? The church associates this gift with baptism, that is, with entering purposely into the death and rising of Jesus. By this participation (which is echoed and nourished in the eucharist) we enter into a new kind of life: death to self, rising to an existence in love. When we can make ourselves radically available to each other, able to enter into communion with each other, then the word of the gospel is being fulfilled in us: "Be opened!"

Twenty-Fourth Sunday of the Year

Is 50:4–9
Ps 116:1–2, 3–4, 5–6, 8–9
Jas 2:14–18
Mk 8:27–35

The notion of "bearing one's cross" is so familiar in Christian piety and spirituality as to be almost a commonplace. If we suffer some particular misfortune or undergo some difficulty, we may see it as our "cross" in life and accept it as a participation in the redemptive suffering of Jesus. Many Christians have been formed in such a spirituality, and have found in it a way of giving positive significance to the otherwise meaningless sufferings they encounter.

While there is certainly a profound validity to this interpretation of the cross in the Christian's life, it must be recognized that it is several steps removed from the original sense of the symbol. In the world of the Roman empire—the world in which Jesus and the early church lived—the cross was not a symbol of life's sufferings, borne with patience; it was a symbol of death—and not simply of death, but of a very specific death: the punishment of a criminal guilty of rebellion against established authority. Crucifixion was not the normal death penalty; it could not be performed on Roman citizens. It was the punishment reserved for those who broke the sacred bond of loyalty: slaves who defied their masters, conquered peoples who revolted against the authority of Rome.

To take up one's cross, therefore, as today's gospel demands, means in the first instance not merely to accept the hardships life inevitably imposes on us, but to bear a kind of suffering which the follower of Christ actively provokes: the Christian must be a rebel against the power and the values of "the world," and must expect to receive the fate reserved for those who defy its authority. The scriptures frequently see human existence as enslaved by powers of evil which control earthly life. The "prince of this world" is the adversary to God; Jesus portrays his mission as a battle to overcome these powers, a revolt against their dominion and the establishment in their stead of the reign of the Father. It is this rebellion which is the more profound reason for Jesus' death on the cross at the hands of the Roman authorities, and his followers must embrace a similar destiny.

The power against which we rebel is not therefore first of all some particular external structure; it is rather the spiritual power of evil which influences every human life by the very fact of being in the world. It is that power which the Christian tradition has frequently called "original sin": the effect and influence of evil on the horizons of our lives prior to any decision on our own part. It comes to us as a part of our heritage as humans, for the world into which we are born already contains the limits and misdirections of human failure and sinfulness and blindness, and it is in this environment that our very selves take shape. To follow Christ, therefore, is to "deny one's very self," and to "lose one's life"; our rebellion is first of all internal, against that power in the self which sets itself up against God: egotism, the tendency to grasp, to manipulate, to subjugate others to our control, to make ourselves an idol.

There is also, of course, an external element to our rebellion. The Christian will always be to some extent in conflict with the values of the surrounding world; the values of Christ will always be to some extent counter-cultural. But the "some extent" is variable. Christ and his message have not been without effect on the world; if our human context is not so hostile to us as it was to our forebears in faith—if none of us is likely to be physically crucified for professing Christ—it is precisely because the establishment of God's kingdom has begun and is underway; the victory over the power of evil has already transformed human hearts—including our own, in baptism—and has established its own structures and community—which we make present in the peace and communion of this eucharist—as a sign of the transformation of the whole world.

Yet this is not a reason for complacency. The letter of James reminds us that faith which does not act in love, meeting the real needs of our brothers and sisters, is without life. It is here that the cross—the punishment for revolt against the world's values—still awaits us. To act upon what we profess as life's true meaning will always mean for us the denial of our very self—that power of autonomy and control—and the loss of its life, for the sake of finding the new life of resurrection. It will always mean judging by different standards of value than those which are superficially attractive. It will always mean a foolish renunciation and loss in the eyes of those who judge by mere human values. We proclaim, after all, a messiah who suffered and lost his life in love for us, who brings God's kingdom through the victory of truth and love. This reality, which we celebrate in the eucharist, confronts us with the imperative of finding expression in the living faith of Christian practice, in the concrete love of our brothers and sisters. It invites us continually to take up this cross—and to find through it the life of resurrection.

Twenty-Fifth Sunday of the Year

Wis 2:12, 17–20
Ps 54:3–4, 5, 6–8
Jas 3:16–4:3
Mk 9:30–37

"Let us beset the just one, because he is obnoxious to us. . . .
With revilement and torture let us put him to the test. . . .
Let us condemn him to a shameful death. . . ."

So speak the evildoers in our first reading, gathering together in their conscious wickedness to plot deviously against the good. A passage in Alexander Solzhenitsyn's *The Gulag Archipelago*, also meditating on the immense and organized evil in the world, might almost have been written in response to this picture:

If only it were so simple! If only there were evil people somewhere insidiously committing evil deeds, and it were necessary only to separate them from the rest of us and destroy them. But the line dividing good and evil cuts through the heart of every human being. And who is willing to destroy a piece of his own heart?

In the second volume of that great book, Solzhenitsyn returns to the same theme:

Gradually it was disclosed to me that the line separating good and evil passes not through states, nor between classes, nor between political parties either—but right through every human heart—and through all human hearts. This line shifts. Inside us, it oscillates with the years. And even within hearts overwhelmed by evil, one small bridgehead of good is retained. And even in the best of hearts, there remains . . . an unuprooted small corner of evil.

Since then I have come to understand the truth of all the religions of the world: They struggle with the *evil inside a human being* (inside every human being). It is impossible to expel evil from the world in its entirety, but it is possible to constrict it within each person. . . .

The liturgy gives us this first reading about the persecution of the just by the wicked as a counterpart to the prediction of Christ's passion in the gospel. But Christian theology has from the beginning also applied to this reality the realization that Solzhenitsyn speaks of: Christ's suffering was not simply the result of the plottings of a group of evil people, but connects with the evil in each one of us. When we say that Christ died "for" the sins of the world, we also mean (theologically speaking) that he died "because of" the sins of the world—including mine.

The struggle against evil, then, means first of all the continual purification of our own hearts. "Who is willing to destroy a piece of his own heart?" Solzhenitsyn asks. Each of us must be willing. The gospel contrasts the prediction of Jesus' death in self-sacrifice with the petty quarreling of the disciples about their relative positions. Jesus' rebuke and his acted-out parable—embracing a little child, a person with no rights or status in society—point to the conversion that must take place in each of us. What do we actually consider most important in life? What do we strive for? We are here to declare and celebrate our belief in the life of love, in communion, in service to all. We do it in the knowledge that there remain in our lives areas perhaps untouched by our faith and commitment, and certainly areas of ambiguity. We do it also in the knowledge that the power of good is ultimately more pervasive and more real in us than that of evil, and in the faith that in every human being there is that power of good, which must be welcomed by us, even if it is now as small and powerless as a child.

Twenty-Sixth Sunday of the Year

Num 11:25–29
Ps 19:8, 10, 12–13, 14
Jas 5:1–6
Mk 9:38–43, 45, 47–48

Autumn seems to be a season in which we are peculiarly aware of the weather. Our consciousness of it is heightened not only by the dramatic changes that take place in nature—like the glorious display of color in the foliage that can be seen in the northern parts of our country—but also by a more ominous yearly phenomenon. This is the season when hurricanes sweep out of the middle Atlantic and wreak havoc along a broad path of destruction. Each year we hear news stories and see TV footage of terrible devastation in the Caribbean islands, and sometimes along our own coast; those of us who live by the seashore have some anxious days every few years as a storm heads in our direction, and we either sigh in relief as it veers out to sea, or we batten down to deal with nature's fury as it passes over us. Rarely, a great storm takes a terrible toll in property and even in lives as it rages through a low-lying area.

For most of us, however, even the worst of hurricanes is unlikely to cause tragedy. At the most, we may go through some inconvenience: flooding of the streets; a few hours or even days without electricity; a disrupting of the normal patterns of life. While a great storm reminds us of our finitude, and shows us dramatically that there are forces beyond our control, it also brings to mind how very sheltered our lives for the most part really are: how infrequently we are exposed to the raw power of nature, how protected we are—as compared with our ancestors and even with our contemporaries in the third world—from accident and misfortune.

The fact that even in the midst of a hurricane most of us can go on living in comfort, in a world of human making, points to a striking feature of the modern world: our technological progress has very largely removed us from frequent experience of the dangerous "limit" situations of life that were so present to previous generations. We are sheltered from storms, inoculated against diseases, cured of illnesses. Science is able to promise most of us a long and reasonably happy life, surrounded by material possessions that would have been the envy of emperors.

All of this, of course, is wonderful. But it also creates something of a problem for us in hearing the gospel in a serious manner; for the gospel's message is about salvation, and most of us live most of the time as though we do not need to be saved—except perhaps in the sense of being guaranteed an afterlife to complete our beatitude.

Today's gospel passage speaks of removing every "obstacle" (*skandalon*) to salvation. The examples given are parts of the body which may lead one to sin or might lead astray any of the "little ones." But for most of us, there are few real "obstacles" in the concrete and particular sense; it is just that nearly *all* of life is lived in a context of forgetfulness of God and the irrelevance of "salvation." Surely if we are honest we must admit that we are in danger of becoming like the rich that the letter of James speaks about: oblivious to the needs of others, living in luxury lives devoid of eternal significance. And yet, what are we to do? Must we deny the world and its goodness? Are we to pluck out the eye for beauty and cut off the hand of work and progress?

A partial answer, at least, is found in what we do when we come together to celebrate the eucharist. Prayer is meant to be for us like a great storm: it removes us from the security of everyday reality and puts us in contact with the sacred, the ultimate limit situation. We are confronted in prayer, if it is genuine, with what we so easily forget: our finitude, our mortality, our kinship with the earth and with each other; our solidarity with all the sorrows and joys of the world; the sense of purpose to life, its beauty and its progress, in the service of others.

But what of the rest of life: those many moments that are not spent in prayer and are devoid of reflection, lived in the habit of secularity? There is some comfort in the words of the earlier part of today's gospel: "Anyone who is not against us is with us." The whole of the secular world is "with" God to the extent that it does not actually lead us away from him; it is with him in secret and implicit ways, in its acts of charity, in its efforts at social order, justice and progress, in its seeking for beauty and truth. Much of what is best in our society is in fact the Christian message of love, appropriated by the world and hidden in secular guise. The Christian's attitude will certainly be to support this reality. But beyond this, there is also another task: to bring to consciousness and reflection the true nature of our world, including its progress and beauty, but also its sorrows and injustice; to overcome the forgetfulness about the purpose of life, and to be for the world a sign of its own deepest dynamism: toward the ultimate meaning and value that we call God and that lives among us by love of one another.

Twenty-Seventh Sunday of the Year

Gen 2:18–24
Ps 128:1–2, 3, 4–5, 6
Heb 2:9–11
Mk 10:2–16

It is one of the joys of the ministry of a priest to be a part of many new beginnings in life, and none is more joyous than the joining of two people who are in love in the bond of marriage. "All the world loves a lover," the old saying goes; and it is easy to be charmed by the enthusiasm and innocence, the fervor and commitment, of young people who have found themselves in each other.

Yet it is hard for a priest today not to think also of the many failures, and to wonder, perhaps even as the couple sits smiling in the office, setting the date for their wedding, whether they will still be smiling so lovingly at each other in five or ten years. Do they really know each other? Is their love real and lasting, or is it a momentary passion or a kind of mutual egotism? Will they too, like so many others, add to the sad statistics on broken marriages? Each of us has seen other unions that began so hopefully and in such joy, only to end in bitterness, recrimination and disillusionment. Indeed, there are few of us today who have not been touched by divorce in our close family or among our good friends. Children of divorced parents are no longer exceptional in our society; their plight is one of the great social problems of our times.

How does faith address such a situation? Our gospel today is of relevance to this concern not so much in giving us a direct answer as in providing a model for thinking about the problem.

The text as we are given it by Mark is already an attempt to apply the morality and insight of Jesus to a social situation in the church which went beyond that of Jesus. It is very likely that the saying about marriage goes back to Jesus himself, but the context in which it is placed is almost certainly from Mark and his awareness of the problems of the early church among the Gentiles. It is unlikely that a Jewish audience would have asked of Jesus so radical a question about divorce, for the simple reason that it was quite clear that the law permitted it (Dt 24:1). The only disputed question among the Jews of Jesus' time was the acceptable grounds: could a man divorce his wife only for unchastity, as the rabbi Shammai taught, or for *any* failure to satisfy her husband, as was the opinion of the rabbi Hillel? Furthermore, Jesus' reply presupposes the possibility of a wife divorcing her husband, as well as vice versa; this, however, was not possible in Jewish law, although it was in Roman law. We have here, then, an adaptation by Mark of Jesus' teaching to the circumstances of Gentile Christians in the Roman empire.

What is the essence of that teaching? Jesus appeals not to the law, but to God's intent. His position is more radical than that of any of the rabbis: he quotes from Genesis to abrogate the rule given (revealed by God, in Jewish belief) in Deuteronomy. In this he reverses a basic idea of his contemporaries' Jewish faith, by claiming that God's earlier revelation was more definitive than the later. Jesus appeals to the creation itself, and to the God-given nature of marriage: the joining of man and wife is the formation of a new reality, a unity which stems from God and must not be broken. (It is also notable that Jesus' statement—at least as reported by Mark—places women on an equal footing with men; in Jewish law, there was a double standard applied, in that a wife could be considered to commit adultery against her husband, but not vice versa; Mark's Jesus however speaks of husbands committing adultery against their wives, thus intimating equality.)

It is clear that Jesus is here, as elsewhere, enunciating the morality of the kingdom of God: how things absolutely ought to be, in accord with God's will. He does not, of course, take into account every situation nor deal with the complexities that face people in their concrete moral choices. The Roman Catholic Church has long recognized, for example, that there are "official" marriages which are not in truth marriages at all, and which therefore can and ought to be dissolved; and there are those who would extend this principle to those who cannot offer juridical proof of the nullity of their relationship. Jesus' words do not simply solve such issues, which involve a context and understanding of marriage itself which was beyond the horizon of either Judaism or the early church.

Nevertheless, even if Jesus' words do not allow us to close off all further discussion, they do tell us something of vital significance: what marriage is meant to be, in the perspective of the ultimate meaning of human existence as given by God. They give us a standard by which to judge not any particular marriage, but the whole context in which our modern problematic arises. There is something wrong with a society in which divorce becomes normal—wrong not simply with marriage, but with our vision of life. Jesus reminds us of the ultimate perspective on all our human relations, of which marriage is the supreme example: "It is not good for man to be alone." We are made for dialogue and sharing of life; and this inevitably means the sacrifice of ego, of the "I," in order to become a large "we." Life makes sense only when we find ourselves in each other, for a purpose outside ourselves. Our vision of "love" must be formed by this standard, not by the superficialities and romances of popular culture. When life itself is seen in this perspective, the perspective of the forgiving, ever-faithful, self-giving love which is given to us, then we can understand the meaning of marriage as a "sacrament" which shows forth exactly what we also celebrate here: the eternal validity of hoping, forgiving, trusting, giving, sharing, because of and for the sake of the communion for which human life is made.

Twenty-Eighth Sunday of the Year

Wis 7:7–11
Ps 90:12–13, 14–15, 16–17
Heb 4:12–13
Mk 10:17–27

During my first year of studies in the theologate, one of my closest friends decided that he would leave the seminary. We had been together for several years, and had shared deeply in a common ideal in aspiring to the priesthood. He had in many ways been an inspiration to me in forming my own vocation, and his friendship had sustained me in many ways. What disturbed me most about his decision to leave, however, was not the fact that we would no longer be together or share the same goal, but that he left the seminary in sorrow. He told me one day that he felt like the rich young man of the gospel, who received an invitation from Jesus but refused it and went away sad. Had my friend said that he felt called to another vocation, I would have rejoiced with him, even though I would miss him; but it pained me to think that he saw his departure as an inability to accept the self-sacrifice demanded, and that the encounter with the Lord left him sad.

In the years since that time, I have realized that there are in fact many people in the situation of the rich young man: people whom the encounter with Christ makes sad. Unlike the man in the gospel, they do not necessarily go away physically; they may remain within the church and even observe its rituals and precepts. They perhaps do not have the honesty or the courage to admit that they would like to go away; but they live the faith begrudgingly, as an obligation and a burden. There is in their religion a lack of joy, enthusiasm, spontaneity, and life, because they see Christianity as an onerous duty rather than as a choice gladly made.

Such an attitude is in striking contrast to the spirit of following Christ we find in the gospels. "Gospel" itself means "good news." The message and call of Jesus should produce joy. His disciples are like the author of our first reading, who considers Wisdom to be beyond all price; health, possessions, and power mean nothing in comparison. Like the characters in Jesus' parables, they joyfully give all they have to gain the one pearl of great price, the unexpected treasure.

But who can rejoice at such a call as that of Jesus—a call to self-sacrifice, service, selfless love, to a life of hope rather than security or possession? To see such a life as "wisdom," as the true meaning of existence, means seeing life in its ultimate perspective, finding what is truly worthwhile; it means facing the deepest issues of life and death, beyond all superficial values. It is for this reason that Jesus' message is addressed to the "poor": those who have nothing to shield them from the problem of human existence, nothing to substitute for the need for God.

This is also why Jesus proclaims that it is difficult or even impossible for the rich to enter God's kingdom—a saying which causes amazement and scandal to the disciples as well as to later Christians. Many efforts have been made to tone down Jesus' statement: for example, reading "cable" (*kamilon*) instead of "camel" (*kamelon*) in the saying about the eye of the needle, or thinking that the latter must have been the name of a narrow gate in Jerusalem (a medieval fancy that modern scholarship deems completely unfounded). But other rabbis also use the same or a similar figure of speech; it is proverbial, and its meaning is clear. Of course, it is an example of semitic hyperbole, the kind of outrageous exaggeration Jesus frequently uses to drive home a point; but that point cannot be escaped. For

Jesus being materially poor does not guarantee entry into the kingdom, but riches are clearly an obstacle.

The reason is also clear. Entering the kingdom means trust in God, not in oneself; even more, it means the *desire* for God: that is, for ultimate reality. This is not the same as the desire for "heaven"; even less is it the fear of punishment either on earth or beyond. These can be simply another form of greed and self-centeredness. What is demanded is desire for *God*—that is, for what ultimate reality is: complete love and self-giving, not in some indeterminate future, but now. The desire for God thus coincides with love of neighbor. (It is notable that Jesus does not tell the rich young man simply to abandon his property, but to sell it and give *to the poor;* it is not a matter of thinking material possessions evil, but of using them correctly.)

This gospel is surely a great challenge to us: to find joy in our faith in the desire to love all people. The words of Jesus do not give us clear and decisive answers to the complex problems of living in the world and using our possessions; we cannot simply read his words to the rich young man as addressed to each of us. But the underlying values are certainly essential for anyone who would follow Jesus; and we must accept this challenge of love, using our hearts and minds to find its application to our lives, if we are not, like the young man, to go away sad.

Twenty-Ninth Sunday of the Year

Is 53:10–11
Ps 33:4–5, 18–19, 20, 22
Heb 4:14–16
Mk 10:35–45

A photograph in the newspaper recently caught my attention. It showed a prominent American cardinal attending a fund-raising dinner in the ballroom of a great hotel. The cardinal, dressed in his full regalia, is shown at the elegant banquet table laughing and conversing with a number of tuxedo-clad politicians and distinguished members of the business community. Perhaps the only remarkable thing about this picture is the fact that what it portrays—the representative of the church quite at home in the midst of money and power—in no way surprises us. We have become used to the fact that the church is a powerful institution, both locally and internationally. Although Stalin laughed at the idea as he asked "How many battalions has the pope?" his successors have seen abundant evidence of the church's power in eastern Europe, especially in Poland, where it is now a major factor in political negotiations. In our own country there are those who would like to see the Catholic Church increase its influence as a political lobby on issues like abortion, school prayer, etc., after the model of some of the fundamentalist churches.

It is of course necessary for the church to speak to the surrounding world and its culture, and to act in an institutional way, as an organized community within the larger society. But there is a constant danger that in doing so the church may end up conforming itself to the institutional models of the world in which it functions. It is common for people not only to think of the church as an institutional power in its relations to society, but also to presume that it is likewise structured internally in the same way as secular society, with its own factions, liberal and conservative, with political maneuvering and patronage, with higher and lower positions, an "old boy" network of connections, promotions and demotions, and all the institutional and human elements of a large and prosperous corporation.

Sadly, this presumption is largely correct. Happily, in most of the world the days are long past when the church could be a profitable "career" with very little requirement of morality or even faith (as was once the case; King Louis XIV, in rejecting a candidate for the primatial see of France, objected that the archbishop of Paris should at least believe in God). But anyone who has experienced the church intimately—especially anyone who has lived for any length of time in the church's administrative center—knows that there is unfortunately still plenty of room for back-biting, factionalism, political intrigue and ambition.

Even more unfortunately, many people actually wish it to be this way. They are comfortable with such structures and motivations in their own lives, and they take it for granted that God works in the same way, but on a larger scale and in a different (but parallel) world. They could not understand and would be very suspicious of a church that renounced the kinds of power, motivations, operations and rewards which they take for granted.

That this is the case should not take us by surprise; apparently Jesus' closest disciples and friends were of the same mentality, as today's gospel shows. In contrast, Jesus proposes a radically different idea of "greatness"—of what is worth striving for. It is the renunciation of power and the aspiration to serve others which must characterize his followers, in contrast with the ways of the Gentiles' rulers. If we take this seriously as a model for the church, it stands as a constant challenge to its leaders and members.

But the import of the message does not stop with its obvious application to the church's authorities. There are those who, renouncing the idea of a church in the image of secular society, think of it instead as a purely otherworldly realm, the exception to the rules of human behavior, a holy society existing over against "normal" life. This idea is also an evasion of the gospel's point. It is not that priests and religious should live generously and in service, while the rest of human society accepts the profit motive and social Darwinism as the legitimate norm of behavior. The message of today's gospel about service is simply an extension of the more general theme so frequently enunciated by Jesus: one must lose one's own life in order to save it; the purpose of human existence can only be found when we have the courage to abandon ourselves in the love of others. This is not a message for the exceptional few who devote themselves to ecclesiastical life; it is the Christian vision of existence. The church is neither to conform itself to the norms of self-seeking secular society nor to be the exception to its rules; it is meant to be the example and the force which transforms the world in *its* image.

Jesus proposes himself—his giving of his life for others —as the model for service. We who commemorate and celebrate that gift in the eucharist are called to live our lives *in* the world in the image of that life given "in ransom for the many."

Thirtieth Sunday of the Year

Jer 31:7–9
Ps 126:1–2, 2–3, 4–5, 6
Heb 5:1–6
Mk 10:46–52

Several years ago when the United Nations celebrated its fortieth anniversary, New York City was filled with world political leaders, dignitaries, and other special visitors who had come for the festivities. It was one of the great ironies of the occasion that the New York newspapers on the day after the anniversary carried under their largest headlines stories not about the observance itself, nor about the speeches and declarations and hopes that marked it, but about the enormous traffic jams that had been caused by the unaccustomed number of vehicles in the U.N. area. The United Nations is an organization dedicated to dealing with the global situation, the widest horizon of human affairs, and its anniversary was the occasion for reaffirming a commitment to attempting to create a vision of the world as a whole; yet what caught people's attention was the local-interest story about a temporary traffic snarl. (In a sense, this might be taken as symbolic of the great dilemma of the U.N. itself; for while it is ostensibly dedicated to a worldwide perspective, its attention has too frequently been focused on the narrow national and local interests of its members.)

It is certainly difficult for human beings to live with the "big picture," to think in terms beyond our immediate interests; in a spiritual sense, to be concerned with the more ultimate and more real. This difficulty is referred to by the scriptures with the image of "blindness," for it is an inability or

113

unwillingness to "see"—that is, to know and understand—what and how the world truly is. There are different forms and levels of spiritual blindness, some more total than others. There is the blindness of egotism, the exclusive concern with one's own person and neglect of the insight that others are equally real and equally valuable. There is the group blindness of prejudice and chauvinism of various kinds, extending even into the attitudes of nations toward one another. There are the small but significant blind spots in our approaches to life, where we frequently prefer not to face the fact of long-range consequences and to see only immediate satisfactions. There is above all the blindness to spiritual reality itself: to our finitude, our sinfulness, and our need for God.

In this perspective the story of Jesus' healing of the blind man has from the earliest times been taken not simply as the account of an individual miracle, but as a paradigm for Christian salvation itself: what Christ does for each of us, opening our spirits to reality. The evangelist emphasizes the blind man's insistent desire to see, his attitude of confidence, his alacrity in coming to Jesus; all these are intended to be examples for us.

But the analogy leaves out an important factor. What blind person would not jump up at the chance of receiving sight? Who would prefer total darkness to the light? And yet in the realm of spirit, we resist, and the reason is plain. We know that the opening of our minds and hearts to the whole truth of being will bring us suffering and loss. In André Gide's wonderful novel *La Symphonie Pastorale* a blind girl brought up by a Protestant pastor receives her sight through an operation, and in her new ability to see discovers for the first time how harsh and ugly the world can be. In her blindness she had been able to live in a lovely world of imagination; in the common light of day, she has to face reality. We have reason to fear that living with spiritual sight, with a vision of the "big picture," with what goes beyond our small world, will bring a demand for compassion and self-sacrifice which go beyond our capacities, will bring an awesome calling which goes beyond our desires.

And yet we are here because, like the blind man, we do want to see; and what we do in the eucharist invites us to a new kind of vision. As Antoine de St-Exupéry said in an oft-quoted phrase, what is most important is invisible to the eyes; we must learn to see with our hearts. In commemorating the death and resurrection of Jesus in a sign of peace and communion, we become open to a new way of seeing with the heart: and what we see is the possibility of a new reality for ourselves and for our world in God.

Thirty-First Sunday of the Year

Dt 6:2–6
Ps 18:2–3, 3–4, 47, 51
Heb 7:23–28
Mk 12:28–34

The wide diffusion of the video cassette player in recent years has been, from the standpoint of a teacher who deals with reading and writing skills, a very mixed blessing at best. One of its benefits, however, has been to make available some of the great film classics which would otherwise be virtually inaccessible to the general public. Among these I recently noted a film which I first saw in the seminary as a theological student: a comedy by the Spanish director Luis Buñuel entitled *The Milky Way*. A surrealistic satire, this film takes the viewer on a highly irreverent pilgrimage through the history of Christian thought and doctrine, pointing out some of its more exaggerated moments. My fellow seminarians and I, being engaged in the arduous study of the same material, found the film hilariously funny.

The history of Christian thought has indeed produced some remarkable aberrations; unfortunately, however, their repercussions have frequently been anything but comic. One of the most significant and influential schools of late medieval philosophy was that of nominalism, which had a pessimistic view of the capacities of the human mind, and emphasized revelation and faith as the only ways of knowing God. Our human concepts do not tell us anything about reality, much less about the reality of God. This doctrine had important theological and ethical consequences. Morality was seen as deriving not from the intrinsic nature of being, but from God's revealed will. Since God was seen as being absolutely free, he could in principle command anything he chose. He could, for example, command that people should hate one another and him instead of loving—and in that case hatred would be virtuous, and love sinful. It is simply a matter of *fact* that God has revealed that he wills us to love; it is his commandment which makes this the center of Christian morality.

As a distinct philosophy, this school of thought is long dead, but its unnoticed influence continues. Wherever we find Christians who have abandoned the mind as a way to God, and attempt to take refuge in a religion of pure positive revelation and law, we may recognize the implied presence and the heritage of nominalism.

For Thomistic theology, on the other hand, the love of God is not a mere command. God *is* love; and in saying this, we are saying something true about the basic nature of his reality and about our necessary relation to it. Our love for God is intrinsic to our very being, and our being reflects the intelligible structure of being itself. God could no more command our hatred than he could will himself out of existence. What God "wills" is the expression of what he *is;* and what God is is also expressed, reflected, and known in what we are.

This way of thinking implies that the total love of God which is the "first of all the commandments" is not an arbitrary law, but is the realization of our inmost being, the fulfillment of our nature. We are made for God; we inevitably love God, secretly desire him, seek for him, even when we stray. It is for this reason that we can and must love God *absolutely:* not as one of the things we love, alongside the others, but as that to which we give our *whole* heart and soul and mind and strength.

This vision also explains why the love of God is intrinsically connected to the love of neighbor: not by a mere linking of two commands, but by the very nature of love. God is not an object among other objects, but is the deepest reality that we love *in* ourselves and in every other being. Just as we are made for God, so also we are made for each other. It is precisely the wholeness of our love of God which makes it all-inclusive; we cannot love God with all our mind and strength unless we love all that participates in his being, all that he loves and creates.

The letter to the Hebrews in today's second reading contrasts the sacrifices of the law with the perfect self-offering of the Son; in similar spirit, the gospel affirms that the love of neighbor is above every ritual sacrifice. It is precisely the spirit of sonship which the "commandments" of love are about. To regard the love and service of God and neighbor as a duty is to miss the point that when we love, we find our true selves. The purpose of God's commands is not the imposition of another's will, but precisely freedom: the ability to will what we truly desire.

Thirty-Second Sunday of the Year

1 Kgs 17:10–16
Ps 146:7, 8–9, 9–10
Heb 9:24–28
Mk 12:38–44

A friend once gave me as a present a record from his collection—a rare one, that could not be replaced. I was reluctant to receive it because I knew that it meant a great deal to him; he not only appreciated the music much more than I, but it also had tremendous sentimental value for him, since it had been given to him by a loved person who was now far away. When I told him I could not take something so significant to him, associated with so many memories, he replied that that was exactly why he wanted me to have it: it meant he was giving not just some thing, but himself.

We live in a world where we are constantly being asked to give: to the church, community funds, hospitals, schools, libraries, museums, public television and radio, the fire department, charities of every kind. Those of us who live in big cities are also likely to be met by scores of people on the streets seeking for handouts. For many of us, such contributions become part of our budget—they are among the "expenses" of living in our kind of society. There is a corresponding danger that such gifts, although still an expression of generosity, become routine and impersonal; they become removed from a commitment of the heart. Moreover, most of us give out of our superfluity, from what we can spare after all our needs and desires are cared for. There are so many requests made of us that this is perhaps to some degree inevitable and necessary; but it may at the limit become so much the routine that it carries over into our very attitude of giving, so that there is no place where we really give ourselves.

A purely material and impersonal giving may even affect our relation to those we should love, and even our giving to God, where the gift of self is all that matters. This is the point of today's gospel, and it reflects similar stories told by other rabbis. One close parallel reads as follows:

> Once a woman brought a handful of fine flour [for a meal offering—Lev 11:2], and the priest despised her, saying: "See what she offers! What is there in this to eat? What is there in this to offer up?" It was shown him in a dream: "Do not despise her! It is regarded [by God] as if she sacrificed her own life." (*Leviticus Rabbah*, III 5)

The gift of the poor is preferred, because they give in real sacrifice; they give from what they live by, and thus give their own lives. The giving of oneself is in God's eyes the most important. And the correlative point is well stated by Ibsen in his play *Brand:* "If you give everything to God, and not your life, you give nothing."

The teaching of Jesus and the rabbis demythologizes the idea of "sacrifice" to God: it is not to be understood as a tribute or a payment or the giving to God of something that he needs or wants for himself (whether his desire be conceived as the food and blood of the offerings of the law or the death of the innocent Jesus as some sort of "payment"). Sacrifice is the symbol of the giving of ourselves; and God wishes ourselves not out of possessiveness, but out of love: for only by giving ourselves to God, for whom we are made, can we *be* our real selves and attain our destined joy.

It is for this reason that the letter to the Hebrews says that Jesus has offered the sacrifice once for all; his relation to the

Father is total giving of self and total receiving from God of life in resurrection; every other self-giving is not something new, but takes part in this one supreme act of love.

But how do we partake in the sacrifice of Christ? This brings us back again to our neighbor. For the Christian, sacrifice is also communion; we give ourselves to God by giving ourselves to each other. We commemorate this liturgically in the eucharist, the whole of which is the "sacrifice of praise," culminating in the union of fellowship and communion. But we share Christ's attitude not only by remembering what he did, but by doing it ourselves, recreating the same attitude in our relations to each other. Our giving to others must be like Christ's giving to us and like our giving to God: not merely paying our dues, but giving ourselves, out of our poverty.

This is a great challenge in a world in which we are the rich—where the danger is one of our being possessed by things, where having creates the feeling of needing more. Meanwhile, the poor widow is multiplied by millions in the slums and villages of the world. Do we have the courage to give not only our aid, but also ourselves?

Thirty-Third Sunday of the Year

Dn 12:1–3
Ps 16:5, 8, 9–10, 11
Heb 10:11–14, 18
Mk 13:24–32

> Some say the world will end in fire,
> Some say in ice.
> From what I've tasted of desire
> I hold with those who favor fire.
> But if it had to perish twice,
> I think I know enough of hate
> To say that for destruction ice
> Is also great
> And would suffice.

Although Robert Frost could not have known it at the time he wrote "Fire and Ice," his poem anticipates the two current physical theories about the end of the universe. Either there is sufficient matter hidden in the cosmos so that eventually the power of gravity will slow down the presently expanding universe and force it to contract in an enormous implosion—ending in an inferno of heat—or there is too little matter, and the expansion which is the result of the "Big Bang" will continue unabated, eventually expending all energy and leaving a frozen, lifeless, infinitely expanding waste.

Whichever scenario one prefers on the basis of current scientific knowledge, one thing is certain: our present universe will end. That point, however, is unimaginably distant in time. Long before then, our sun will have expanded to become the kind of star known as a red giant, swallowing up all the planets as far as the orbit of Jupiter. By that time it is likely that the human race will already have been long gone—most probably extinct, but if not, then changed by evolution to something entirely beyond our ken.

Such predictions from science have radically altered humanity's perspective on itself. At one time it was presumed in the western biblical outlook that humanity—even though created on the "sixth day" according to Genesis—was present virtually from the beginning of the world, and would be present until its apocalyptic end. We now know that humanity has been on earth for only a few moments on a geological time scale, and that the earth's own existence is a recent event in cosmic history. Such considerations—which have long been part of the outlook of religions like Hinduism and Buddhism—lead to speculation about the possibility of other life and intelligence in the vastness of space-time, and also to a sense of humility about our own place. They also expose the naiveté and inadequacy of systems of thought—like that of Marx and Engels—that propose some future earthly utopia as capable of giving total meaning to human existence; for, apart from the death that each individual must face, we know as well that the whole of the human race must one day die, and our entire physical universe end, whether in fire or in ice.

What of Christian eschatological expectations? The main point of the theological idea of "the end" is not a prediction about the physical fate of the universe, or even of the earth, but a conviction that human history has a culmination in God. It is true that Jesus seems to have thought—and the early church certainly did—that an apocalyptic ending of the world, with the coming of judgment (as in the reading from Daniel) and the establishment of God's kingdom, would take place shortly. Against this must be set Mark's including an admission by Jesus of his own ignorance of the time of judgment. In any case, the final word concerning the coming of the kingdom is not contained in what Jesus said or thought during his ministry, but in the fact of his resurrection. It is this event which interprets the "end time" for us: whenever the physical end of the world may come, we *now* are called to live the life of God's kingdom, that is, to live in intimacy with God and with each other, and to bring about within the present world not only the longing for, but the sign and presence of, God's final peace and love toward all beings.

Thirty-Fourth or Last Sunday of the Year—Feast of Christ the King

Dn 7:13–14
Ps 93:1–2, 5
Rev 1:5–8
Jn 18:33–37

We celebrate this Sunday the feast of Christ the King. The notions of the "reign" of God and of the kingship of Christ are not only crucial to Christian spirituality and imagination, but are intimately tied with the entire context of the gospel proclamation—to the extent that the title "Christ the King" is in fact a tautology, since the word "Christ" translates the Hebrew and Aramaic words for "messiah," which signifies God's "anointed"—i.e. the king of Israel.

But exactly what is the meaning of this so-familiar designation? In what does the "kingdom" of Christ consist if—as the gospel tells us—it "does not belong to this world"?

In the second reading for the feast we are given a series of titles which connect the "kingship" of Christ with his death, resurrection, and future coming. He is the "faithful witness": as the gospel also indicates, Jesus' task is to testify to the truth, even to the point of death; and his death *is* in fact the witness to God's love and the world's rejection. He is "the first-born of the dead": the one in whom death is transformed into life, not only for himself, but for his many brothers and sisters. He is the "ruler of the kings of earth": the one in whom history will find its goal, and whose power will overcome even those who now persecute the church. He is pictured coming on the clouds, like the mysterious Son of Man in the prophecy of

Daniel (first reading), to be given everlasting dominion, even over those who once put him to death.

And yet his kingdom is not of this world. The rule of Christ is not an exercise of power, in the normal sense of the word, but it teaches us the true nature of power and of rule. His "almighty power" is not that of force, but that of truth and love. It did not save Jesus from the cross, nor the church from persecution; it is not a power which imposes itself on the world to subdue it, but it gives the world hope for its future. (For this reason, even while being involved in the transformation of society, the church must always resist the temptation to identify itself or its mission with the "powers" of this world or with any particular political program; much less may it offer itself as a theocratic alternative to civil authority.)

The kingdom of Christ is by its nature invisible; it cannot be on the same level as the powers of the world. When we say in the eucharist, "the kingdom, the power, and the glory are yours, *now* and forever," we are making an act of faith, not an empirical observation. It is only by faith and hope that we can distinguish the reign of God in history; for what presents itself plainly is the reign of suffering and sin. What is *visible* in history is the cross, not the resurrection.

Nevertheless, the kingdom of Christ is not a purely future reality; in the theological language of John's gospel, it is "not here," but it is *now*. It is the reality which allows us to transcend the merely empirical dimension of life and to live in joy despite life's tragedy and limitation. For this reason the Christian gathering is called "thanksgiving," eucharist, and consists in communion and the giving of peace.

In our secular society, we also celebrate in this season a feast of Thanksgiving—a day of remembrance of God's benefits. The eucharist teaches us that it is right to give thanks "always and everywhere"—not simply for the "good things" that we receive from God, but for all of life, even for the cross itself; for we recognize in ourselves the triumph of God's love, the kingdom which we await "with joyful hope," and make present by our very act of hopeful waiting.